D0588472

This book is due for return on or before the last date shown below.

railway.com

Parallels between the early British railways and the ICT revolution

ROBERT C. B. MILLER

The Institute of Economic Affairs

First published in Great Britain in 2003 by
The Institute of Economic Affairs
2 Lord North Street
Westminster
London SW1P 3LB
in association with Profile Books Ltd

The mission of the Institute of Economic Affairs is to improve public understanding of the fundamental institutions of a free society, with particular reference to the role of markets in solving economic and social problems.

A CIP catalogue record for this book is available from the British Library.

ISBN 0 255 36534 9

Many IEA publications are translated into languages other than English or are reprinted. Permission to translate or to reprint should be sought from the Director General at the address above.

Typeset in Stone by MacGuru Ltd
info@macguru.org.uk

Printed and bound in Great Britain by Hobbs the Printers

CONTENTS

THE AUTHOR

Robert Miller is a graduate of the Universities of Dublin and Edinburgh and is a financial journalist and consultant. He is a former Senior Research Fellow of the Institute of Economic Affairs and was the author with John Wood of *Exchange Control for Ever?* (1979) and *What Price Unemployment?* (1982) for the IEA. He was also the author for the IEA of *State Forestry for the Axe* (1982) and *A Market for Access to Lloyd's Syndicates?* (1989). He has been a consultant to a number of City institutions, including the London International Financial Futures and Options Exchange, International Commodities Clearing House and the International Underwriting Association of London. He is currently a consultant to the Association of Lloyd's Members, the trade association of private capital in the Lloyd's insurance market. He contributes regularly to the *Fleet Street Letter*, the *Nikkei Shimbun*, and to the specialist reinsurance press.

He is married with two grown-up children and spends his time in London and Wiltshire. He is currently planning a history of the Lloyd's crisis of the 1990s.

FOREWORD

railway.com, IEA Research Monograph 57, is an important contribution to economic thinking. It draws on a detailed, yet absorb-
ing, analysis of the economic history of the early British railways
revolution and the information and computer technology (ICT)
revolution to develop lessons for policy-making in areas such as
regulation, government intervention in infrastructure projects
and financial markets. The author also draws a number of lessons
that help our understanding of the role of markets in conditions
that are far from the idealised model of perfect competition that is
generally presented in economic textbooks.

Both railways and the Internet are two-way networks and
both developments revolutionised communications. The dawn of
both technologies was accompanied by a widespread belief that a
'new economy' was developing, with a step-change in productivity
likely. In both cases, this belief led to a stock market boom, and
then a subsequent collapse when investors realised that the likely
increase in productivity could not justify share prices at levels seen
at the top of the boom.

Miller demonstrates that it would be dangerous to try to prevent such stock market bubbles, even if that were possible. They
are part of the discovery process of the market which helps to
determine which companies and technologies are most valuable.
We cannot know the best way of doing things until the market has

experimented, as Miller says, 'The resources expended by the failed businesses are no more wasted than the efforts of scientists applied in the falsification of a scientific theory' (Introduction). Furthermore, Miller argues, the railway and Internet bubbles ensured that the process of experimentation was concentrated in a short time. It also seems clear from the evidence that the consumer was the main beneficiary of any misallocation of capital as such misallocation led to denser networks, greater competition and lower prices.

The 'problem' of technological 'lock-in' is often cited as a reason for government intervention when networks develop. If governments do not intervene and choose the 'best' technological standard, the market can become 'locked in' to an inferior standard, it is frequently argued. This is relevant in the development of the railways (the broad gauge versus standard gauge debate) and the development of computing systems (for example, competition between Apple Macintosh and Microsoft). Miller argues convincingly that there is no 'lock-in' problem. Markets do not choose obviously inferior technologies. More importantly, he makes a point that is not widely understood. Competition between technologies, before one of them becomes dominant, ensures that all the potential technologies are more effective than an imposed monopoly standard would have been. EU experience in imposing technological standards for the 3G mobile phone network has not been successful, argues Miller.

There are many other lessons for public policy to be drawn from an analysis of the railway and ICT booms. For example, markets can order the most complex of economic processes very effectively. Implementation of railway through-ticketing and the standardisation of time on our clocks did not need a 'fat controller' in Whitehall, merely the subtle interplay of market forces.

Closed-form economic theorising and econometric modelling may well play an important part in helping us to understand the workings of a market. However, the diminution of the importance of economic history in economics teaching and higher study means that an important method for improving economic understanding is in decline. Miller uses that method – the study of markets in an historical context – very effectively in Research Monograph 57.

The views expressed in Research Monograph 57 are, as in all IEA publications, those of the author and not those of the Institute (which has no corporate view), its managing trustees, Academic Advisory Council members or senior staff.

PHILIP BOOTH

Editorial and Programme Director
Institute of Economic Affairs
Professor of Insurance and Risk Management,
Sir John Cass Business School, City University
July 2003

ACKNOWLEDGEMENTS

The author is grateful to the following for permission to reproduce material: Alan Sutton, *American Economic Review*, Cambridge University Press, Chatto & Windus, Federal Reserve Bank of St Louis, *Financial Times*, *Harvard Business Review*, Macmillan, *Newsweek*, Oxford University Press, Penguin, *Regulation*, and Smithers & Co.

He is particularly grateful to Professor Robert M. Schwartz of Mount Holyoke College for supplying the maps in Figure 4 and to Simon Morrison of the Falkland Press for skilfully adjusting them.

Finally, he is grateful also to his mother, Mrs L. M. Miller, for the reference to the Brontë sisters' railway investments, and to his family for their tolerance of an enthusiasm for early British railways.

The front cover

The front cover shows J. M. W. Turner's picture *Rain, Steam and Speed*, and is reproduced by permission of the Trustees of the National Gallery. The picture, painted in 1844, the year before the peak of the 'large' railway mania, shows a train crossing the Maidenhead bridge over the Thames on the Great Western Railway main line between Bristol and London.

SUMMARY

- There are strong 'homologies' (significant structural similarities) between the early British railways revolution and the more recent information and communications technologies (ICT) revolution.
- Both industries involved the development of two-way networks and considerable network economies and also heralded a revolution in communications.
- There are also strong economic and financial similarities between the two revolutions. Both were accompanied by a stock market bubble, an increase in economic growth and considerable investment in the new technologies. In both cases, the magnitude of the impact of the new technology on productivity was ambiguous but the direction was not.
- The 'bubble' that accompanied the developments in railways and ICT was part of the market discovery process. Whilst a 'perfect world' would not have involved such a bubble, a perfect world cannot be created by government intervention.
- The development of financial and investment 'bubbles' had some benefits. They ensured that the process of market discovery was concentrated in a short period. Consumers were beneficiaries of the 'bubbles', even if investors lost money.
- Where governments have played a dominant role in

technology revolutions, outcomes have been inferior to the outcomes of free markets. Examples include French government intervention in the nineteenth-century railway system, which was subject to inefficiency and under-provision, and EU intervention in the case of 3G mobile phone networks.

- It is clear that, even in unsophisticated economies, markets are effective at ordering very complex processes.
- Important policy issues arise from network revolutions, such as the degree of government coordination that is appropriate and how technology standards should be chosen.
- Experience of the market 'choosing' standards or technologies has not led to inferior technologies being 'locked in'. On the contrary, competition between technologies has led to improvements in all competing standards and it is often some time before the market determines a dominant standard.
- Many lessons can be drawn from an analysis of the development of the railways to help us understand the likely future course of the ICT revolution.

TABLES AND FIGURES

railway.com

1   INTRODUCTION

The early British railway and information and computer technology revolutions

This monograph explores the parallels between the development of the early British railways (EBRs) in the mid-nineteenth century and the information and communications technology (ICT) revolution of the late twentieth and early twenty-first centuries. It attempts to show that there are large structural similarities, or homologies, between the EBR and ICT revolutions and that consequently the development of the former can provide insights into the latter. Both developed under conditions which, to a remarkable degree, were free from direct government intervention. In addition, both revolutions involved communications networks, and as a result they have many similar economic characteristics.

An important reason for comparing the two revolutions is that the railway revolution occurred sufficiently long ago – the British railway network peaked at about 20,000 miles in the early 1900s – that it is possible to see the history of the system from the seeming fantasies of early visionaries to maturity. As a result it is possible to identify stages in its development which result from its character as a mature network that the ICT revolution has yet to reach. For example, given a competitive framework it is likely that the high profits of companies initially developing the network will be reduced by competition despite the existence of network externalities. Network externalities are the increasing returns that result from the additional value that network users gain the more the network is used.

Another reason why the railway revolution is important for understanding the ICT revolution is that the former involved two boom and bust cycles, one small in the 1830s and another much larger in the 1840s. In particular, the 'large' railway mania of 1845 and the stock market collapse and recession that followed it throw light on the ICT bubble, which peaked in 1999 and 2000.

One contemporary issue on which the EBR revolution can also throw light is the so-called 'Solow productivity paradox', which asserts that the evidence for computers is 'everywhere except in the productivity statistics'. The paradox was highlighted as long ago as 1987 by the economist Professor Robert Solow, in an article in the *New York Review of Books*.[1] More recently it has been used as a label for the issue of whether the surge in US productivity growth in the second half of the 1990s was apparent or real, and whether it could be ascribed to the ICT revolution or some other cause. An examination of the history of the EBR revolution cannot decide the issue by itself, but it does suggest why the effect of the new ICT technology might be delayed and why a 'Solow productivity paradox' is likely to emerge with the development of any major new technology.

---

1   Robert Solow, 'You can see the computer age everywhere but in the productivity statistics', *New York Review of Books*, 12 July 1987.

Parallels in economic history: analogies and homologies

But how useful are parallels in economics? Can the history of one period be used to draw lessons for another? Financial journalists and academics use historic 'varieties of economic experience' to interpret current economic events, but usually they restrict their examples to the comparatively recent past and to relatively short-lived phenomena, such as overvalued exchange rates and the inflationary consequences of monetary expansion. But the drawing of parallels between much larger, longer-lasting and more complex phenomena is more difficult. The parallel between, say, the quarter-century-long railway revolution in Victorian Britain and the equally long ICT revolution comes into this category. But one way to ensure that correct lessons are drawn from a historical parallel is to find experiences which have most in common – so that it is more likely that the experience of one period can provide useful insights into the other. This monograph argues that the EBR and ICT revolutions have more in common than other parallels with the latter, such as the nineteenth-century development of the telegraph or the creation of the US electricity supply industry in the late nineteenth and early twentieth centuries. But this is not to say that these less satisfactory parallels are not superior in some respects. For example, the development of the US telegraph network resembles more closely the virtual networks of computer operating systems because the cost of entry is low compared with railway networks.

In the early 1960s, NASA commissioned a study on the parallels between the development of the railways in the United States and the space programme.[2] In the introduction, Professor Mazlish

---

2   B. Mazlish (ed.), *The Railroads and the Space Program: An Exploration in Historical Analogy*, Cambridge, MA, and London, 1965.

explores the distinction between an analogy and a homology. He defines analogies as representing superficial resemblances while the latter represent deeper structural similarities. This monograph draws out the 'homologies' between the EBR and ICT revolutions to explain how features of the ICT revolution flow from its structure and are not merely incidental.

Lessons for public policy

Given the homologies to be described in Chapter 2, the experience of the EBR and ICT revolutions have some important lessons for public policy. These include the following:

Consumers not shareholders benefit if networks are built by private enterprise

An examination of the history of the EBRs suggests that the regime of free enterprise, remarkably similar to that which has governed the ICT revolution, allowed entrepreneurs to equip Britain with a railway network that was denser and built earlier than those of other nations. For example, by 1870 Britain had a network that had more line per square kilometre and per capita than France; and most important, all at no expense to the taxpayer, whereas in France the taxpayer had to reach deep into his pocket from the start. It is a commonplace (or more likely a misconception) of economic history that the laissez-faire development of the EBRs in the 1830s, 1840s and 1850s was chaotic and was accurately characterised by the phrase 'wasteful competition'. But the evidence suggests that the apparent chaos masked a process that led to the larger proportion of returns from the new technology accruing to consumers rather than shareholders. While some shareholders got hurt in the rough and tumble, in most cases severe losses were limited to shareholders in the highly speculative companies that emerged in 1844 and 1845. It is clear that, despite much contemporary (and later) criticism, there is no evidence that the system could have been improved by the centrally planned system that operated in France. While no one currently suggests that the networks of the ICT revolution should be administered by the state, there is still a strong belief that they should be guided by government intervention. The evidence of railway network development in Britain and France in the nineteenth century does not support this view.

Saving the taxpayer from the effects of appraisal optimism

Indeed, it can also be argued that the development of the British railway system in the last century offers a model for major infrastructure projects today. The private enterprise regime of the mid-nineteenth century ensured that the extra costs of the perhaps inevitable 'appraisal optimism' of the very large projects involving new technology were borne by the shareholders – and not taxpayers. That large projects often suffer from cost overruns is a commonplace, but recently Bent Flyvbjerg, Nils Bruzelius and Werner Rothengatter have documented just how frequent and how large are such misjudgements when major projects are completed.[3] It is significant that the vast majority of the projects they describe are public sector, taxpayer-financed projects. But the development of

3   Bent Flyvbjerg, Nils Bruzelius and Werner Rothengatter, *Megaprojects and Risk: An Anatomy of Ambition*, Cambridge University Press, 2003.

the EBRs shows how the private enterprise development of such projects has an inbuilt correction device. If there are large cost overruns then the shareholders revolt as they must bear the losses. What is more, shareholders tend to be better equipped to accept the risks inherent in such projects than taxpayers. Investors are volunteers, taxpayers are conscripts.

New technology, economic statistics and economic policy

Another important issue for public policy raised by the parallel between the EBR and ICT revolutions is that technology revolutions can create distortions in economic statistics that make economic and monetary policy-making more than usually difficult. In the case of the EBR revolution, the difficulty only appeared long after the event, when the economist Gary Hawke attempted in the 1970s to estimate the 'social savings' that resulted from the introduction of the railways. The issue turned on whether railway passenger travel was to be valued as the equivalent of 'inside' or 'outside' seats in a coach. Such was the difference in price between the two that, depending on which was chosen, GDP was enhanced by as little as 2 per cent or as much as 5.5 per cent. A similar problem led to the establishment of the Boskin Commission in the USA in the mid-1990s to reassess Consumer Price Index (CPI) statistics on the grounds that they did not properly measure improvements in computer technology. If CPI figures are distorted by new technology then so are GDP and productivity statistics. The lesson is that policy should not be too dependent on such macroeconomic statistics, and the danger of such dependence is especially serious in times of rapid technological change.

Bubbles – the discovery process of the market

The development of new technology has been associated with stock market bubbles. The analysis of this paper, drawing on both the EBR and ICT bubbles, is that to a large degree the bubble in the share prices of the new technology companies is the market process of trial and error which sorts out which companies are workable businesses from those that are not. It follows that the dot-com and telecom bubbles were not just 'cons', and that the resources used up were not wasted. Without perfect foresight, the trial-and-error process that involves companies raising money and attempting and failing to establish profitable businesses is the only way to discover how the new technology can serve consumers. The resources expended by the failed businesses are no more wasted than the efforts of scientists applied in the falsification of a scientific theory.

New technology bubbles can be exacerbated by monetary and financial mismanagement. In such cases, the experimental discovery process is damaged and entrepreneurs have the extra burden of dealing with misinformation introduced into the system by a mistaken government or central bank policy. In the 1990s, excessive optimism was induced by the so-called 'Greenspan put', which led to the belief that the US stock market would not be allowed to fall significantly and that any weakness would be met by interest rates cuts by the Federal Reserve. This had the effect of creating an aura of unwarranted optimism similar to that described by 'Austrian' theorists. Austrian economists argued that the upswing in the trade cycle is caused by the central bank imposing interest rates lower than the undistorted market or 'natural' rate; entrepreneurs are deceived into thinking that there are more resources available than is actually the case. In turn, this causes exaggerated optimism and over-expansion which are frustrated when the required complementary resources turn out not to be available. That development of a new technology is possible without a bubble is demonstrated by the introduction of electric light and power in the first decades of the last century.

'Lock-in': a new kind of market failure?

It has been argued by some economists, for example Brian Arthur and Paul Krugman, that the special economic 'winner takes all' character of the development of networks means that 'inferior standards', such as Microsoft Windows or QWERTY keyboards, can be 'locked in' merely because they were first on the scene. Other economists have disputed the existence of this kind of apparent market failure. They have pointed out that it assumes that consumers are largely passive and incapable of collaborating to replace an inferior standard. They also question the assumption that the Windows operating system and QWERTY keyboards were inferior products. The development of the EBRs was marked by competition between standards – the broad gauge, which was used by the Great Western Railway (GWR) and its allied railway companies in South Wales and the west of England, and the standard gauge, which was employed everywhere else. The history of the replacement of the broad gauge illustrates the means by which consumers can collaborate to replace one standard by another.

It might be thought that the selection of a universal standard, such as a railway gauge or 3G mobile phone technology, should best be undertaken by government. But this assumption seems misplaced. The European Union (EU) appears to have selected such a high standard for 3G mobile phones in the EU that introduction of the technology in Europe may have been delayed. The evidence is that consumers and producers of such standard services are quite capable of selecting the standard that suits them best. Intervention by government may be unnecessary at best, or harmful at worst.

Another lesson of the EBR revolution is that the market is capable of resolving problems of coordination thrown up by the new technology. The difficulty of 'through-ticketing' for journeys over the lines of more than one railway company was solved by the creation of the Railway Clearing House, which ensured that companies were paid according to distance covered on each of their lines. Such solutions show how, given a satisfactory institutional framework, the market is capable of selecting appropriate standards and changing them if and when they prove unsuitable. An interesting ICT example is the World Wide Web Consortium, which has established standards and protocols for use on the World Wide Web. The ability of the market to develop such standards is also demonstrated by the emergence in the EBR revolution of uniform 'railway time', which was necessary for train timetables and to make a railway network workable.

Synopsis

The remainder of the monograph is structured as follows. In Chapter 2, it is argued that the parallels between the EBR and ICT revolutions are more numerous than the parallels with other technological revolutions, which are less illuminating in most respects. In Chapter 3, the fact that both EBR and ICT revolutions involve networks and network economics is explored. It is argued that competitive development forces business to adopt similar strategies. ICT companies, such as Vodafone and Apple, are compelled by the logic of network economics to adopt similar strategies to those used by EBR companies such as the London & North Western Railway (L&NWR) and the GWR. Chapter 4 describes the parallels between the EBR and ICT revolutions in terms of their effect on productivity and economic growth. Chapter 5 examines the parallels between the railway manias of the 1830s and 1840s and the ICT bubble of 1999 and 2000. Chapter 6 explores the arguments of the 'path dependence' theorists, who claim that second-rate technologies can get 'locked in' by being first on the scene, and argues that such 'lock-ins' are unlikely to occur as there are market mechanisms that can be used to achieve changes in network standards. It follows that government intervention to prevent lock-in is misplaced. Chapter 7 comprises a summary and conclusion.

Annex: a note on prices

To give an indication of the current (2003) value of money amounts in the 1835–55 period, contemporary amounts of money have been multiplied by 50. This procedure gives an inevitably imprecise result for two reasons. First, there have been large changes in relative prices; for example, labour has become much more expensive and communications much less. Second, over the 1835–55 period prices fluctuated, with periods of falling prices being succeeded by periods of rising prices and then falling prices again – see the following table. The solution has been to use a multiplier of 50 throughout to give a rough-and-ready indication of the 2003 equivalent of Victorian monetary values; £100 then was worth £5,000 today.

Multiplier to obtain 2003 values

1835	51.9
1840	41.5
1845	49.5
1850	55.1
1855	41.9

Source: Data for the period 1270–1914 has been taken from E. H. Phelps Brown and S. V. Hopkins, 'Seven Centuries of the Prices of Consumables, compared with Builders' Wage-rates', *Economica*. Data after this period has been taken from the Office of National Statistics.

An attempt has also been made to give an indication of the scale of some of the railway projects by taking their costs as a percentage of contemporary GDP and then expressing it as a percentage of UK or US GDP in 2002. GDP in 2002 has been assumed to be $10,000 billion for the US and £1,500 billion for the UK.

For example, the initial estimate of the cost of the Grand Junction Railway was £1 million in 1833, when its authorising Act was passed. In that year UK GDP was £412 million, so the projected cost of the railway from Birmingham to Liverpool was 0.24 per cent of GDP. The cost of a project equal to 0.24 per cent of UK GDP in 2002 would have been £3.6 billion. The equivalent figure for the US would have been $24 billion. This illustrates the size of the projections in current amounts – compare with the £5.8 billion cost (2003 prices) of the Channel Tunnel and the $14 billion cost of the Boston 'Big Dig' road tunnel.

2 THE EARLY BRITISH RAILWAY AND ICT REVOLUTIONS

Two communications revolutions

In December 2000, *The Economist* began publishing a regular supplement called 'Technology Quarterly', focusing primarily on new developments in information and computer technology. The supplement's first editorial, entitled 'In praise of disruption', explained that innovation was responsible for more than half of productivity growth. One article queried, 'Is Bluetooth worth the wait?', and another reviewed IBM's plans to build the world's most powerful computer.[1]

In October 1845, *The Economist* began publication of a supplement called 'The Railway Monitor', which was to survey developments in the new technology of the time – railways. This weekly supplement carried a listing of railway share price movements, published the Board of Trade's 'railway traffic returns', and reported on railway company meetings. Its first issue reviewed the history of railways to 1845 and speculated on the benefits that they were likely to have for the economy and productivity. It commented:

> A man can accomplish now in a day what he could not do
> thirty years ago in three or four days. The labour, therefore,
> of the whole population is thus rendered infinitely more

---

1   *The Economist Technology Quarterly*, December 2000.

productive; and it is so far exactly in effect what it would be if we increased enormously the productive population of the country without increasing its number of consumers.[2]

In both 1845 and 2000, *The Economist* was responding to the excitement created by the dramatic development of new technologies that promised to transform the economies of advanced countries. Both involved communications technology and, as we shall see, 'two-way' networks which have similar economic characteristics that make their development by businesses in competition very similar.

Further, in both 1845 and 2000 the revolutionary possibilities of railways and computer networks inspired what the economist Robert Shiller has described as 'new era' thinking that accompanied the stock market booms of the mid-1840s and late 1990s. In his book *Irrational Exuberance*, Shiller described how in the late 1990s there was much enthusiasm for an apparent 'new era' of prosperity which legitimised the high stock market.[3] He argued that such views are often held in periods when stock markets show 'irrational exuberance', and cited the early 1900s and the 1920s as other periods when such 'new era' thinking prevailed.

A similar episode of 'new era' thinking was experienced in Britain in the mid-1840s, based on the new technology of the railways. The railway historian John Francis, writing in 1851, cited a number of commentators who were extravagant in their 'new era' thinking;[4] for example:

---

2   *Economist, Railway Monitor*, 4 October 1845, p. 952.

3   R. Shiller, *Irrational Exuberance*, Princeton University Press, 2000.

4   J. Francis, *A History of the English Railway*, vol. II, Longman, Brown, Green, & Longman, 1851, pp. 140ff.

Railways are the wonder of the world. Nothing during the last few years has created so marvellous a change as the great iron revolution of science ... Other revolutions have scattered luminous influences over the world, but it remained for the new generation of railways to bring about one of the mightiest moral and social revolutions that ever hallowed the annals of any age.

The enthusiasm for railways described by John Francis compares with that of Louis Gerstner, Chairman of IBM, for the ICT revolution. In testimony to Congress in 1999, he said:

We are witnessing nothing less than the rise of a digital economy and a new global medium that will be the single most important driver of business, economic and social change in the coming century.[5]

In explaining the 'irrational exuberance' of the stock market in the late 1990s, Shiller argued that because the Internet was 'a source of entertainment and preoccupation for us all', it was easy to believe that it was of great economic importance.[6] It was easier, he claimed, to imagine the consequences of advances in Internet technology than those in shipbuilding or materials science, which are not so visible to ordinary people. The advent of the railways was also highly visible, and its importance was obvious. Charles Dickens, in *Dombey and Son*, which was written soon after the 'large' railway mania of the 1840s, described how important the railways had become in early Victorian England.

5   Quoted in K. L. Kliesen and D. Wheelock, 'The Microchip Flexes Its Muscle: Can It Compare with History's Best?', *The Regional Economist*, Federal Reserve Bank of St Louis, July 2001.

6   Shiller, op. cit., p. 19.

There were railway patterns in its drapers' shops and
railway journals in the windows of its newsmen. There were
railway hotels, office-houses, lodging houses, boarding
houses; railway plans, maps, views, wrappers, bottles,
sandwich boxes, and railway time-tables; railway hackney-
coach and cab stands; railway omnibuses, railway streets
and buildings, railway hangers-on and parasites, and
flatterers out of all calculation. There was even railway time
observed in clocks, as if the sun itself had given in.[7]

In the 1830s and 1840s, Isambard Kingdom Brunel, Joseph
Locke and Robert Stephenson were the early Victorian equivalents
of Bill Gates, Michael Dell and Andrew Bezos. In February 1833, at
the age of only 26, Brunel was appointed the engineer to the GWR,
which was to run from London to Bristol at an estimated cost of
£2.5 million (£125 million in approximate 2003 values). This huge
project eventually cost over £6 million and was completed in 1841.
(This latter figure would be equivalent to perhaps £18 billion in
terms of the same proportion of 2002 UK GDP.) Similarly, at the
age of 30, Joseph Locke replaced his mentor, the railway pioneer
George Stephenson, as the engineer for the Grand Junction Railway between Birmingham and Liverpool. This project, which cost
over £1 million (£50 million in approximate 2003 values), linked
the world's first long-distance railway, the Liverpool and Manchester, with the London and Birmingham Railway.

---

7   Charles Dickens, *Dombey and Son,* Penguin Classics, 1985, pp. 289–90. The book
     was first published in nineteen monthly instalments between October 1846 and
     April 1848.

The origins of the EBRs

The EBRs originated in the wagon ways, or tramways, used in the coal industry, and it was only with the construction of the Stockton & Darlington Railway (S&DR) that it was discovered that railways could be used for passengers and general freight. The S&DR was launched in 1825 as a line designed to carry coal some 30 miles from collieries south of Durham to Stockton on the coast so that it could be transported by ship to London and elsewhere. The intention was to reduce the exorbitant cost of moving coal from the colliery to the coast. The S&DR's authorising Act of Parliament followed the pattern of those for turnpike roads and canals. While the S&DR was free to operate its own vehicles on the railway, it had to permit the owners of other vehicles to use it on payment of a toll. The result was that the railway was used in a variety of different ways. Most of the traffic was pulled by horses, and while a large proportion of the trains were owned by the S&DR itself, individual colliery owners used their own wagons and horses. It was also used for passenger traffic, and two lady publicans ran horse-drawn carriages. The result was a combination of chaos, invention and success. The railway was built as a single track with passing places, and as traffic increased there were queues (and disputes) for their use. Light passenger coaches were supposed to give way to heavier coal trains. The locomotive engines introduced under the guidance of George Stephenson confirmed that mobile engines were at least as good as suppliers of motive power such as horses or stationary engines hauling wagons by ropes. The success, both technical and commercial, of the S&DR demonstrated for the first time that railways could have a commercial use beyond coal and mineral traffic in the north-east of England.

The discovery that railways could be highly profitable for transporting goods generally, not just coal and people, was made by the Liverpool and Manchester Railway (L&MR), which set the pattern for all other railways. Like the S&DR, the L&MR was established to break the stranglehold of a monopoly canal which took an indirect route between the two cities. The result of the monopoly was that the rapidly expanding cotton trade was faced with massive transport costs between its main centre, Manchester, and its chief port, Liverpool. As a consequence, and in what was to become the traditional fashion, the businessmen of the two cities, Liverpool merchants and Manchester mill owners, collaborated to build a railway between the two centres. An Act was passed in 1826, and the railway was opened in September 1830. Almost immediately upon completion, the L&MR was carrying mail, road 'containers' for Pickfords and had begun passenger excursions. From the start the proportion of passenger traffic was far larger than had been expected. It rapidly became clear that there were very large profits to be made, and that passengers as much as freight would be responsible for profitability. By the end of 1830, 70,000 passengers had been carried by the L&MR, and between 1831 and 1845 passengers accounted for 56 per cent of its total traffic receipts.[8]

The result of these early developments was the investment of £193 million (approximately equivalent to £9.7 billion in 2002 values) in railways between 1830 and 1850, culminating in the two railway 'manias' of 1837 and 1845 discussed in Chapter 5. The total was equivalent to 36 per cent of UK GDP in 1850.

---

8   See the article 'Passenger Train Traffic' in J. Simmons and G. Biddle (eds), *The Oxford Companion to British Railway History*, Oxford University Press, 1999.

Networks: the link between the EBR and ICT revolutions

Real and virtual communications

The railways and the ICT technologies have the shared characteristic that they are both communications systems. Communications systems naturally divide into two types. *Physical* communications allow for the transport of people and objects from one place to another. *Virtual* communications involve the transmission of text, images or sounds separately or in combination. Physical communication tends to be interactive: anyone attached to the network can communicate with anyone else similarly attached. Thus all Londoners can use the Underground system to visit each other, if they wish. Similarly, businesses can use air transport to send goods to each other; any business that has access to an airport can send goods to any other business in a similar position.

But this interactive feature of physical communications is not shared with many forms of virtual communication. Some communications systems, such as radio and (terrestrial) television, do not have this interactive feature. Only the central nodes of the network can transmit information, and likewise they cannot receive it. Others on the network can receive communications, but cannot send them. ICT technologies, such as the Internet and telecoms, involve numerous virtual two-way interactive communications systems.

Interactive communication – two-way networks

A characteristic shared by the ICT and EBR revolutions is that they both involved the development of two-way networks. Networks have special economic characteristics which make their development different from that of other technical innovations.

These network effects mean that the law of diminishing returns is suspended (for a time), and that increasing investments in the network bring larger rather than smaller returns. This reflects the fact that, for instance, the more mobile phone users there are, the more useful a mobile phone becomes. Similarly, as the size of a railway system and the number of stations increases, the number of possible journeys increases disproportionately. These economic characteristics are shared by railways and important parts of the ICT revolution. While the network characteristics of the Internet and telecoms are obvious, they also apply to software in virtual networks. The more people use the Windows operating system, the greater the benefits for each user; not only will the software become cheaper, but advantages will stem from widely dispersed knowledge about the operating system and how to use it.

The economics of networks and 'network externalities' are discussed in Chapter 3.

General-purpose technologies

One striking parallel between the EBR and ICT revolutions is that they were both general-purpose technologies (GPTs). In other words, they could be applied in a wide variety of different ways; for example, they both involve customer-to-customer 'C2C' and business-to-business 'B2B' communications. Both the EBRs and information and computer technology have developed considerable importance for the economy generally after an embryo stage when they were of relevance only to specific industries. In the case of the EBRs and the Internet, the importance respectively of passenger traffic and the use of the Internet by the general public caused surprise.

The discovery that a technology that was used in an obscure branch of the coal and iron trade in the north-east of England could bring about large savings in costs for industry and business generally has parallels with the development of B2B and business-to-customer (B2C) traffic on the Internet, which began as a computer link between American defence and academic institutions. As in the 1830s and 1840s, when business discovered the costs of physical communication could be reduced by railway transport, so in the 1990s information and computer technology was seen as a way of reducing business costs and improving the quality of the service provided.

Economists have argued that GPTs themselves create spill-over effects in the form of increasing returns to scale, and that these operate to increase productivity growth. But these are separate from the network externalities discussed above and in Chapter 3. The economists Timothy Bresnahan and Manuel Trajtenberg have argued that GPTs have the function of 'enabling technologies' that increase productivity downstream from the original innovation.[9]

An example of the enabling character of the EBR and ICT revolutions is that both permitted the development of marketplaces. One of the great successes of the Internet has been the development of auction sites, such as Ebay, which allow users to buy and sell almost anything in a convenient way that was much more difficult before the development of the Internet. In a similar way, the

---

9   T. F. Bresnahan and M. Trajtenberg, 'General Purpose Technologies: Engines for Growth', *Journal of Econometrics*, 65, 1995, pp. 83–108, quoted in David A. Paul and Gavin Wright, *General Purpose Technologies and Surges in Productivity: Historical Reflections on the Future of the ICT Revolution*, Symposium on Economic Challenges of the 21st Century in Historical Perspective, Oxford, July 1999, p. 14.

growth of railways led to the development of markets for produce and livestock adjoining stations, which displaced or transformed traditional markets. For example, in the 1870s cattle markets were built in Leicester and York served by branch lines. And Smithfield meat market in London, which was built in the late 1860s, had a goods station in its basement served by the GWR and the Metropolitan Railway.[10]

EBR and ICT: unregulated revolutions?

Laissez-faire in Britain

The EBRs were developed in a laissez-faire regime with very little economic regulation. Railways in most countries other than Britain were subsidised almost from the outset, with governments planning routes, guaranteeing interest or dividends and soliciting investors to build and construct them. Often, this was in reaction to what was perceived as the 'chaotic' British system with its 'wasteful' competition, but it had the effect of protecting shareholders and leaving the countries in question with networks less dense than the British. The economic historian T. R. Gourvish, in his analysis of the railways and the British economy, described the laissez-faire regime as follows:

> In the United Kingdom the creation of the early railway
> network, from the choice of routes and the raising of capital
> to the operation of services, was left to private enterprise.
> The sole restraint on the free market was imposed by the

---

10   See the articles 'Markets and Fairs' and 'Meat Traffic' in Simmons and Biddle, op. cit.

private act procedure of Parliament, which required each new project to pass the scrutiny of committees of both Houses before obtaining powers to purchase land, and to raise capital under conditions of limited liability.[11]

Suspicion of government interference meant that regulation was strictly limited. The Railway Regulation Acts of 1840, 1842 and 1844 prescribed minimal economic regulation and required only that new railways had to be certified as safe by Board of Trade inspectors and that railway companies made statistical returns. The only attempt at economic regulation occurred in 1844 with the passage of Gladstone's Act. The 1844 Railway Regulation Act, steered through parliament by Gladstone as President of the Board of Trade, allowed for the eventual nationalisation and for the compulsory provision of cheap 'parliamentary' trains. The clauses allowing for nationalisation were fiercely resisted by the railway companies and were never put into effect. Under the Act, the government could nationalise railway companies established after 1845 after the lapse of 20 years for an amount equivalent to 25 times the companies' average profits for years 18, 19 and 20.

The requirement of the 1844 Railway Regulation Act that five Board of Trade officials, the 'railway kings', should examine each proposed railway bill was ineffective in limiting the flow of railway bills and was discarded in 1845. Both the House of Lords and the House of Commons showed scarcely restrained enthusiasm for authorising new railways, including those that were in competition with previously authorised lines. Having authorised a line,

11   T. R. Gourvish, *Railways and the British Economy 1830–1914*, Macmillan Press, 1980, p. 49. (Reproduced with permission by Palgrave Macmillan.)

there was nothing to stop Parliament authorising competing lines at a later date, and this regularly happened, forcing many railway companies to spend large sums in attempting to prevent their authorisation.

The individualist British framework is remarkably similar to that now governing the development of many of the real and virtual networks of the ICT revolution. It follows that the effects of competition on the development of the EBRs can have lessons for the ICT revolution. Much contemporary and later criticism of the competitive 'chaotic' character of the EBR private bill system of authorisation now appears misconceived. In contrast to Europe and the USA, where railways were often subsidised, the private bill system provided Britain with a railway network at negligible cost to the taxpayer. In addition, the British network was denser and developed more rapidly than those of other countries. It is also revealing that many of the critics of the British system complained that competition was damaging to the interests of railway shareholders, but not that it provided an inadequate network.

Not laissez-faire elsewhere

In the USA, the development of railways followed quickly after their introduction in Britain but took a different course. The Baltimore and Ohio Railroad was authorised in 1828 only three years after the opening of the S&DR in 1825. Railways were heavily subsidised by government, and it has been estimated for the eleven states of the south of the USA that 55 per cent of the cost of all railway construction before 1861 was contributed by taxpayers. There was also significant state involvement in the northern states. Of the four main lines that reached Lake Erie or the Ohio river by 1855, public authorities had provided well over half the funds for three of them. For the USA as a whole, it has been estimated that some 30 per cent of the total cost of railway construction before the Civil War was provided by public state, local and federal governments.[12] The development of the American railroads also offers a less precise parallel with their British counterparts, because the former were in competition with an expanding American canal system. In Britain canal building ceased with the advent of railways, but in America it continued. Between 1830 and 1850, canal mileage in the US more than doubled from 1,277 to 3,698, while that of railways increased from 73 to 8,879. Competition from canals, other waterways and from 'blue water' shipping remained important in the United States.[13]

In France the development of a national railway system was planned and in part financed by the state. The French government decided routes, retained the right to purchase the companies and supervised rates and charges. It also imposed safety precautions and had the right of representation on railway company boards.[14] Under a law of 1842, nine networks (later reduced to six) were established centred on Paris, and the government selected which companies were to obtain the 99-year franchises after which the railways would become the property of the state.[15] No competing parallel lines were built and French governments frequently guar-

---

12 C. Goodrich, *Government Promotion of American Canals and Railroads 1800–1890*, Columbia University Press, NY, 1960, pp. 270–1.

13 R. W. Fogel, *Railroads and American Economic Growth*, Johns Hopkins Press, 1964.

14 M. Robbins, *The Railway Age*, Routledge & Kegan Paul, 1962, pp. 144–5 & 150.

15 K. A. Doukas, *The French Railroads and the State*, Columbia University Press, 1945.

anteed interest payments. In Prussia, the government guaranteed the interest payments of railway companies and built the 'Eastern Railway' linking Berlin and the agricultural eastern provinces with the Rhineland and Westphalia. In other European countries, state control and subsidy were important in the development of national railway systems, often for strategic reasons.[16] Even in Ireland, the government made loans to railway companies, and in India the Governor General, Lord Dalhousie, who, as vice-president of the Board of Trade under Gladstone, had considerable experience of the laissez-faire development of railways, imposed a system similar to that in France. The government selected the routes and then allocated them to railway companies.

The laissez-faire ICT revolution

While the development of the railways in the nineteenth century was carried out with a considerable degree of state planning and subsidy in most countries except for Britain, the ICT revolution has so far involved little government intervention. The limited exceptions have been the anti-trust suits in the USA against Microsoft (see Chapter 6) and the auctions for the 3G radio spectrum in Europe (see Chapter 3), although in the latter case there are parallels with the private bill procedure for the authorisation of the EBRs. Nonetheless, in the main the ICT revolution has been largely free from direct government intervention and subsidy – like the development of the railways in mid-nineteenth-century Britain.

---

16 E. A. Pratt, *The Case against Railway Nationalisation*, Collins' Clear Type Press, n.d., pp. 12ff.

Stock exchange bubbles

Both the EBR and the ICT revolutions were accompanied by stock market bubbles. In the case of the EBR revolution there were two bubbles, the 'little' and the 'large' railway manias which peaked respectively in 1837 and 1845. In both cases, there was wild speculation in railway shares and, particularly in the 'large' mania of the 1840s, there was the extravagant promotion of new railway lines that turned out to have little immediate prospect of success. In this respect the 1845 railway mania was remarkably similar to the Internet and telecom bubble of 1999 and 2000. A contemporary historian, John Francis, quoted a report from *The Bankers Magazine*:

> … we are to have railway streets in London, with carriages over-head and the foot-passengers and shopkeepers underneath; while in the country railway steam-engines on the atmospheric plan are not only to perform all the work of the lines, but are to employ their surplus power in impregnating the earth with carbonic acid and other gases, so that vegetation may be forced forward despite all the present ordinary vicissitudes of the weather, and corn may be made to grow at railway speed.[17]

There were, for example, schemes for 'direct lines' between cities that already had connecting indirect links; these included a Cambridge and Oxford line and a Bristol and Liverpool line, which incorporated a bridge over the Avon at Aust near Bristol. There was even a scheme for a round-London 'M25' line, the Metropolitan Junction Railway. Frequently, there were several companies all seeking parliamentary authority for the same route. This speculative frenzy was paralleled by the excesses of the ICT bubble

---

17   Francis, op. cit., p. 143. For details of atmospheric railways, see p. 55 below.

in 1999 and 2000. Bubble companies such as E-toys and Boo.com were often competing for the same franchise or competing with established businesses that would have little difficulty in establishing Internet offshoots.

But the 'large' railway mania of the 1840s (and to a lesser extent the 'small' mania of the mid-1830s) shared an important characteristic with the ICT bubble of 1999 and 2000. They all involved a high degree of popular interest in and excitement about the new technology which were believed to have important economic and social consequences. The economist Robert Shiller has argued that such public knowledge and enthusiasm have been a major factor in sustaining the 'irrational exuberance' of the late 1990s. It was certainly the case in the railway manias of the 1830s and 1840s.

Figure 1 shows how the large railway mania of the 1840s compares with the ICT bubble of the late 1990s. The figure shows the index of railway shares from May 1827 and December 1859 with the NASDAQ index of predominantly US technology shares overlaid, so that the peak of the 'large' railway mania of July 1845 coincides with the peak of the ICT bubble in March 2000. It is evident that, while there are significant similarities between the two stock market bubbles, there are also two important differences. First, as we have seen, there were two railway manias, the 'little' in the 1830s and the 'large' in the 1840s. So far there has been only one ICT bubble, although a second is not impossible. Second, the ICT bubble of 1999 and 2000 has seen share prices rise and fall farther and more rapidly than was the case in the 'large' railway mania of the 1840s. In the three years prior to their respective peaks the NASDAQ and the EBR share indices increased respectively by 284 and 87 per cent. In the three years following their respective peaks the NASDAQ and EBR indices fell respectively by 72 and 40 per

Figure 1   **GRS railway shares and NASDAQ**

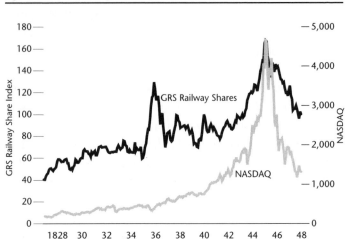

Sources: GRS Railway Share index May 1827–December 1859 – see Annex to Chapter 5, pp. xxxff; NASDAQ February 1982–February 2003.

cent. However, the EBR index eventually reached a low point in October 1849, down 64 per cent from its July 1845 high.[18]

New technology and the macroeconomy

Effect on productivity: a Victorian Solow Paradox?

It was claimed contemporaneously that both the EBR and the ICT revolutions had a significant effect on productivity growth. In the

18   The GRS Railway Share index probably underestimates the volatility of railway shares generally as it includes the shares of a small number of established railway companies and excludes those of the bubble companies – see the Annex to Chapter 5.

case of the EBRs it was only in 1970 that an attempt was made to estimate accurately the effect of the railways on the British economy in the nineteenth century. The economist G. R. Hawke estimated that in 1865 the EBRs saved between £43 million and £76 million, or between 4.9 and 8.7 per cent of UK GNP, but settled on the higher figure as the most likely.[19] But the precision of this estimate has been called into question by the economic historian T. R. Gourvish,[20] who has argued that, on realistic assumptions, the range of possible savings was much larger. He estimated that the EBRs might have saved between 2.0 and 16.8 per cent of GDP, but settled for an intermediate position of a saving of about 10 per cent. This figure is similar to Hawke's preferred higher estimate, and is supported by the nineteenth-century economist Dudley Baxter, who calculated in 1866 that savings derived from the EBRs would have been £72 million or about 8.3 per cent of GDP.[21] This range of social savings results in large measure from the different possible values given to passenger traffic. Should transport in a railway carriage be valued the same as 'inside' or 'outside' seats on a stagecoach? This problem of valuation is inescapable in assessing the impact of any new technology. How is the progression from Windows 95 to Windows XP to be valued for the purposes of GDP statistics?

Another parallel between the EBR and ICT revolutions is that the former involved an equivalent of the 'Solow Productivity Paradox', which, as we have seen, asserts that the evidence of

---

19 Hawke, op. cit.

20 Gourvish, op. cit., pp. 58–9.

21 D. Baxter, 'Railway Expansion and Its Results', *Journal of the Statistical Society*, vol. XXIX, 1866, reprinted in E. M. Carus-Wilson (ed.), *Essays in Economic History*, vol. III, 1962.

computers is everywhere except in the productivity statistics. Until the spurt in productivity growth in the late 1990s in the USA, it puzzled economists that the seemingly pervasive use of computers had had negligible effect on the productivity statistics. Explanations for the paradox included the argument that the production statistics failed to record the benefits of the use of computers. Here there is a striking parallel with the inability of economists to estimate the value of the benefits that should be attributed to the railways. But also there is evidence that the effects of the railways on the economy were slow to take effect; it took some time for people to learn how to use the new technology and for the skills needed to diffuse through the economy. A similar drawn-out process of learning how to use the new computer technology has been suggested to explain (away) the Solow Productivity Paradox.

How important was the EBR revolution in mid-nineteenth-century Britain compared with the ICT revolution in late twentieth-century America? According to three LSE economists, between 1974 and 1995 the effect of the ICT revolution on US economic growth was 0.75 per cent per annum, three times that of the effect of the EBRs between 1840 and 1870.[22] While the difference is large and both figures are subject to a wide margin of error, they show that the effects on productivity of the two revolutions were of the same order of magnitude.

Another important conclusion can be drawn concerning the collapse of the ICT bubble in 2000 and the crisis of the 'new economy'. The collapse of the railway bubbles in the 1830s and the 1840s did not mean that the EBR revolution was of only minor im-

---

22 D. Baines, N. Crafts and T. Leunig, *Railways and the Electronic Age*, www.fathom.com, 2001.

portance to the economy. Although some of the wilder optimism of the bubble years was misplaced, the impact of the railways on the Victorian economy was substantial. Similarly, the bursting of the ICT bubble in 2000 does not mean that the ICT revolution is an illusion with only minor long-term effects.[23]

A nineteenth-century recession in the twenty-first century

The second parallel between the economic effects of the EBR and ICT revolutions is that they may have been significant factors in causing recessions. Many commentators claim that the current slowdown in the USA is the result of an excessive, or misdirected, investment boom in ICT technology. In the same way, it is claimed that the economic crisis and recession of the late 1840s were the result of over-investment in railways. Most economic historians accept that the recession of the late 1840s in Britain was the result of the collapse of the railway boom of 1844–6. On the other hand, there is no evidence that the recession of the late 1830s was the result of the collapse of the 'little' railway mania in 1837.

Economists seeking an example of a nineteenth-century recession to help understand any recession resulting from the bursting of the ICT bubble need look no farther than the economic crisis of the late 1840s in Britain.

---

23 This appears to be the conclusion of John Cassidy. In his book, *dot.com* (Allen Lane, The Penguin Press, 2002), he argues that the dot-com bubble was a complete illusion; but see Chapter 5, pp. 160ff, 'EBR and ICT bubble companies', for a contrary view.

New technologies from the leading economies

Both the EBR and ICT revolutions originated in the larger and most advanced economies of their respective times. The new railway technology developed in Britain, which was the second-largest economy in the world between 1820 and 1850 (after France). Table 1 compares the GDP of Britain and other leading economies in 1820 and 1850. It also shows how Britain was by far the largest producer of pig iron and cotton goods, illustrating Britain's position as the leader in the development of new technology. Also shown is the length of railway line in use in 1840 and 1860.

Table 2 shows equivalent statistics for the ICT revolution. The position of the USA as the largest and most advanced economy and as the leader in the ICT revolution is evident.

That the new technology should be developed by the most advanced and largest economies of the time is no surprise. Only the richer countries have the technological skills and the surplus resources that enable a country to afford the trial-and-error process involved in the development of new technologies where costs, practicability and profitability are all highly uncertain. In both the EBR and ICT revolutions the full effects and consequences were very unclear at the outset. Only the richest countries can afford to take the risks involved in the process of experimentation that determines which of the available technologies will succeed. Furthermore, the conditions that lead to general economic growth are likely to be the same as those that lead to the nurturing of new technologies.

Nineteenth-century globalisation

One important factor shared by the EBR and ICT revolutions is that

Table 1   **Economic leadership and the EBR revolution**

Country	Length of railway line open (miles) 1840	Length of railway line open (miles) 1860	Annual output of coal and lignite (metric tonnes) 1840–44	Cotton spindles ('000s) 1834	GDP 1820 (millions of 1990 Geary-Khamis $)	GDP 1850 (millions of 1990 Geary-Khamis $)
Austro-Hungary	90	2,839	0.5	800		
Belgium	209	1,081	4.1	200	4,433	8,042
France	310	5,729	3.5	2,500	38,071	60,685
Germany	293	6,931	4.4	626[a]	16,393	29,449
Great Britain	1,494	9,127	34.2	10,000	34,829	60,479
Italy	13	1,503			22,042	
Netherlands	11	209			3,677	5,844
Russia	17	1,016	–	700[b]		
Spain	–	1,198				
Sweden	–	329			3,098	4,490
USA	3,326	30,636			12,432	42,475

a 1836   b 1840

Note: Although France was (just) the largest economy in both 1820 and 1850,
Britain was also significantly ahead of France in terms of GDP per capita:

	1820	1850
France	$1,259	$1,675
Great Britain	$2,500	$2,926

(1990 Geary-Khamis $)

Sources: A. Maddison, *Monitoring the World Economy 1820–1992*, OECD,
1995; *Modern History Sourcebook*; *Spread of Railways in the 19th Century*
(www.fordham.edu/halsall/mod/infrev6); B. R. Mitchell, *International Historical
Statistics*, Europe 1750-1993, 4th ed., Macmillan, 1998.

Table 2   **Economic leadership and the ICT revolution**

Website visits August 2000: GDP 2000					
Country	GDP $ trillion	Visits: GDP ratio	Country	GDP $ trillion	Visits: GDP ratio
US	9.8	76	Germany	1.9	8
Japan	4.8	16	Brazil	1.3	8
Canada	0.7	12	Australia	0.4	6
UK	1.4	10	France	1.3	4

Sources: Website visits; *Financial Times* Special Report: 'The Internet Revolution: lies,
damned lies and web valuations', 13 October 2000, p. 16; GDP: OECD; CIA World
Fact Book.

they both took place at times of increasing 'globalisation'. In other words, both revolutions took place when trade liberalisation made it easy for international trade to expand. In the 1990s, the movement towards freer trade culminated in the formation of the World Trade Organization (WTO), which replaced the General Agreement on Tariffs and Trade (GATT), and the extension of trade liberalisation to services. It also saw the move towards both Russia and China joining the WTO. In the 1840s, the free trade movement achieved its most significant success with the repeal of the Corn Laws in 1846, admittedly as a direct result of the Irish famine. But other tariffs were reduced on goods imported into Britain, although they remained high on exports to other countries in the 1840s and 1850s. Nonetheless, the mid-nineteenth century was a period when international trade increased dramatically; the real value of world exports multiplied eight times between 1820 and 1870.[24]

In capital markets too there are significant similarities between the two periods. In the 1990s capital could move freely between the major economies of the world. Exchange controls existed in no major economy, and investors were free to invest where they chose with the ability to repatriate capital whenever they wished. The 1840s were remarkably similar. There was an extensive market in London for foreign securities. J. H. Clapham describes the international, even global, character of the London capital market in the following way:

> [In the 1830s] ... American railroad bonds and continental
> railroad shares began to attract the investing public. Some
> of the French and Belgian companies were half English in
> capital management and design ... By August 1845, regular

---

24   A. Maddison, *Monitoring the World Economy*, OECD, 1995, Table I.4.

quotations in financial newspapers included the stocks
of most European and of many South American states; of
thirteen of the United States, one of which – Pennsylvania –
had six separate issues listed; of the United States Bank and
the Bank of Louisiana; of half-a-dozen colonial joint-stock
banks and of the bank of the Ionian Islands; of New Orleans
and New York cities; the bonds of the Camden and Amoy
and of the Philadelphia and Reading railroads, with the
shares of eight French railways, one Belgian railway – the
Sambre and Meuse – and the Dutch-Rhenish railway.[25]

Clapham further explained that by 1847 the number of foreign
railways quoted in London had risen to 34, of which fourteen were
French. There were quotations for Indian and Canadian lines, the
Great Indian Peninsula and the Great Western of Canada, and for
railways in Spain, Ceylon and Jamaica – the Jamaica South Midland Junction.[26]

But in addition to supplying capital, Britain also exported
railway technology and expertise, although this diminished with
the passage of time. The first French railways depended heavily
on British engineers for their design and British navvies for much
of the unskilled work. In similar fashion, the early American railways used British engines and rails. It has been calculated that in
the periods 1844–51 and 1852–9, 8 and 6 per cent respectively of
total British pig-iron production was exported for foreign railway
construction.[27] Here the parallel with the international reach of
American computer software and hardware companies is clear.

---

25   J. H. Clapham, *An Economic History of Modern Britain, The Early Railway Age
      1820–1850*, Cambridge University Press, 1950, pp. 493–4.

26   Ibid., p. 494.

27   Gourvish, op. cit., p. 24.

Competing technologies: no dominant patent

The EBR revolution involved competing and evolving technologies and was not dominated by a few patents or patent holders. The ICT revolution is similarly free from dominating patents. A number of other major technological innovations have involved a small number of patents that have allowed patent holders to dominate the new industries. In the case of the EBRs, Richard Trevithick's patents for locomotive engines, granted in the early years of the century, had expired, so that by the 1830s and 1840s locomotives could be used without the need to pay royalties to patentees. Thus George Stephenson's combination of tubular boiler and blast pipe as used in the *Rocket* in the Rainhill trials of 1828 could be freely adopted by other railways.

This freedom from dominant patent holders is also true of the ICT revolution. While patents and copyrights protect particular innovations, in the main they are limited in scope, so that in many cases equivalent products can be developed. For example, although the Netscape Web browser is protected by copyright, it did not prevent the development of Internet Explorer, which had the same function. In very few cases do major ICT patent or copyright holders have a dominant position in the market. This is in contrast to the development of the telegraph industry, where a few patentees charged royalties to telegraph companies for the use of their patents. The early electricity industry was organised in a similar way with the ownership of the patents, direct-current Edison or alternating Westinghouse, charging the generating and distribution companies for the use of the patents. The early US telegraph industry was racked by disputes between patentees and the operating companies, which had to pay to use the patents.

It is interesting that this might not have been the case. In the 1830s and 1840s, the now completely forgotten technology of atmospheric railways was supported by many experts, including Isambard Kingdom Brunel, Michael Faraday and the railway economist Dr Dionysius Lardner, as providing traction superior to that of steam locomotives. Had various technical problems been resolved, atmospheric railways might have operated successfully as commuter lines and in suburban and national networks. It was only for technical reasons that the EBRs were not dominated by patentees like the American telegraph and electricity industries.

Accounting fraud: WorldCom and George Hudson

One important 'homology' between the EBR and ICT booms is that they both ended in accounting scandals that appear to have similar causes. In 1849 George Hudson, the 'railway king', was forced to resign the chairmanships of the companies that he controlled because of a series of accounting scandals and malpractices.[28] A series of revelations about his companies, including the Midland

---

28 It has been claimed that in his novel, *The Way We Live Now*, Anthony Trollope based the character Augustus Melmotte on Hudson. But Brian Bailey has pointed out that Trollope, writing in the 1870s, more than twenty years after Hudson's fall, probably based his character on Albert Gottheimer, who had interests in railways and mines and had acquired a fortune by dubious means. Dickens' character Mr Merdle in *Little Dorrit* appears to have been based on the career of the Irish MP John Sadleir, which ended in financial scandal and suicide. However, Mr Vigo in Disraeli's last novel *Endymion* was almost certainly based on Hudson, as he was a Yorkshireman, chairman of the Great Cloudland railway and involved in railway projects in Yorkshire and Lancashire. See B. Bailey, *George Hudson, The Rise and Fall of the Railway King,* Alan Sutton, 1995, pp. 160ff, 'George Hudson in Fiction'.

Railway, the York Newcastle and Berwick, the York & North Midland and the Eastern Counties, exposed the payment of dividends out of capital and the purchase of shares from Hudson by the York and North Berwick at far above their market price.[29] In the case of the Eastern Counties Railway, over a period of three years more than £200,000 in dividends was paid out of capital. *The Observer* commented on the report of a committee of inquiry into the York and North Midland Railway:

> For four years, thirteen millions of capital, the property of the company in question and its alliances, have been at the mercy of Messrs. Hudson and Waddington, with which they actually did as they chose, making and unmaking dividends, traffic, capital, and revenue, just as they pleased, disbursing sums of which they refuse to render any account, pocketing cheques for which there is no authority, and of which they will give no explanation; appropriating to themselves money belonging to the company: and even descending to the petty meanness of making the company pay their hotel expenses.[30]

The Hudson scandals are very similar to those associated with the American telecom company WorldCom in 2002, when it was revealed that profits had been overstated by $3.8 billion.[31] The managers of WorldCom had recorded ordinary expenses as capital expenditure and consequently had boosted the company's apparent earnings. Both the Hudson railways and WorldCom had found themselves in very similar difficulties. Because of rapid expansion as a result of attempting to exploit communication

29   Bailey, op. cit., pp. 92ff.
30   Quoted in ibid., p. 100.
31   'WorldCom crisis hits markets', *Financial Times*, 27 June 2002.

networks, both Hudson and WorldCom were faced by the same 'if you're not in, you can't win', 'winner takes all' demands of the competitive network development. In other words, companies are forced to expand aggressively to establish themselves because failure to expand risks possibly serious, even fatal, competitive disadvantage – see Chapter 3.

Other possible parallels

The ICT revolution has led a number of writers to seek parallels in economic and business history with similar technological changes. Each explains some features of the ICT revolution, but none shares as many 'homologies' as the development of the EBRs. For example, it has been suggested that the development of the US electricity industry might offer parallels with the ICT revolution.[32] Although electricity requires networks for its delivery, these are one-way distribution networks which do not involve communications. Nevertheless, the development of electricity networks did have a significant effect on business costs, and electricity is supplied both to consumers directly and to business. Both the development of the interstate highway system in the US and the ICT revolution involve the creation of networks, but there are major differences. The interstate highway system was planned, built and financed by the government. The capital was raised by the US government on the security of its revenues and there was no equity investment in the projects.[33]

---

32   P. A. David, *Computer and Dynamo, The Modern Productivity Paradox in a Not-Too-Distant Mirror*, Warwick University, July 1989.

33   The building of the interstate highways has been called 'interstate socialism'.

Tom Standage, in his book *The Victorian Internet*, has described the development of the telegraph in the nineteenth century, and there is an obvious parallel between the development of the telegraph and the Internet and mobile phone networks.[34] There are, though, some significant differences. As we have seen, the telegraph was based on a limited number of patents, those of Morse and Hughes, for example, and led to tension between the owners of the patents and the licensees. In contrast, both the EBR and ICT revolutions have been largely free of such controversies. Nonetheless, there are some interesting parallels with the ICT revolution, as the sunk costs of developing a telegraph network were low (between $50 and $100 a mile) so the costs of entry were also low and competition was intense. The competition between the different networks using the different telegraph patents parallels both the broad gauge/standard gauge division in the EBRs and the Apple/Microsoft division in the ICT revolution.

However, the major difference between the development of the telegraph in the United States and the EBR and ICT revolutions is that there was a rapid process of amalgamation which led to the elimination of competition and the formation of a nationwide monopoly by Western Union at the end of the American Civil War in 1866. In most other countries, the state played a dominant role as the telegraph was of great military importance.

Comparing the EBR and ICT revolutions

There are, though, major differences between the development of the EBRs and the ICT revolution. But these differences do not

---

34   T. Standage, *The Victorian Internet*, Phoenix, 1998.

detract from the usefulness of the parallels in extrapolating from the development of the EBRs to the ICT technologies.

No hardware/software distinction in railways

Perhaps the most significant difference is that in the case of the railways there was no clear parallel with the hardware/software distinction that is so pervasive in ICT technology. The railways came largely hard-wired. The railway equivalent of software is engine and rolling-stock technology, but in contrast to computer technology in general and the Internet in particular, once the initial development of effective locomotives had taken place in the 1820s, innovations were largely improvements in speed and haulage capacity. Perhaps there is a 'homology' between the introduction of locomotives and the development of the Windows graphics user interface (mouse, 'point and click'), which was launched in the mid-1980s as part of Windows 1.0, but since the basic design of a railway system was settled only incremental improvements have taken place.

Multiplicity of ICT networks

The ICT revolution involves a multiplicity of networks while the EBRs were limited to two physical networks, reduced to one in 1892 following the conversion of the GWR's broad-gauge lines to standard gauge. In contrast, the ICT revolution involves a large number of different networks, some of which are physical. These networks include the Internet, the World Wide Web and mobile phones. Others networks are virtual networks. Computer operating systems, such as Microsoft Windows, like other networks, involve increased value to users as the standard is more widely adopted. Many of these networks are at different stages of development – some are in their infancy while others are mature.

Conclusion

The EBR and ICT revolutions have a number of important characteristics in common. One major difference, the multiplicity of networks in the ICT revolution compared with the single national rail network, makes it easier to draw conclusions from the EBRs and apply them to the ICT revolution. The single railway network makes it possible to isolate the factors that governed the competitive process and to apply them to the separate ICT networks. The development of other networks does not offer as many points of resemblance with the ICT revolution as do the EBRs, although in some cases they can offer insights into the ICT revolution.

3 RAILWAYS AND OTHER NETWORKS

Network economics, the EBRs and ICT revolutions

There are various aspects of network economics which should be considered when analysing the EBR and ICT revolutions. We first analyse the nature of networks and how they involve 'network externalities'. The effects explain many of the homologies between the development of the EBR and ICT revolutions. We then describe how increasing returns follow the building of the connections between the most important nodes of the network, but not later, less important connections – the application respectively of Metcalfe's and De Long's laws. This analysis is applied to the development of the EBRs in the 1840s and 1850s and to aspects of the ICT revolution.

Real and virtual networks

Railways exclusively involve 'physical' networks, whereas ICT technologies involve both 'physical' and 'virtual' networks. A 'physical' network connects a number of nodes, such as stations in the case of railways, so that objects or information can flow from one node to any of the others. Telegraph or telephone systems are physical networks as messages can be sent from each participant to any of the others, across the cables that make up the network. A 'virtual' network, on the other hand, has many of the same characteristics as a 'physical' network despite there being no physical links between the members of the system. Virtual networks require standardised technology which makes it possible for the system to be used by large numbers. Examples include the VHS video standard and the different versions of Microsoft Windows. Neither standard requires a direct physical connection, but users of both systems benefit directly from there being a large number of other users. And the greater the universality of the standard, the greater the value to each individual user.

The ICT industry involves a number of connected physical and virtual networks. Computers of all kinds, the Internet, the World Wide Web and 3G telephony consist of a number of related real and virtual networks. Virtual networks include the operating systems that have made the ICT revolution possible and the software that makes it useful. Physical networks, in contrast, involve the connections that make communications possible.

The Windows operating system has become almost universal despite competition from the Apple standard and more recently from Linux. The survival of the Apple standard is probably explained by it being especially suitable for publishing and graphics, and by the ability to transfer documents and files between Apple and Windows programmes. Nonetheless, the software remains incompatible, and a programme that works on an Apple PC will not work on Windows and vice versa.

Tim Berners-Lee, the founder of the World Wide Web, chose this term for the interactive communications network he planned because the word 'web' is used in a mathematical context to describe a network of nodes all of which can be connected with each other.[1] And the description applies equally to any physical or virtual network as well as to the World Wide Web.

Network externalities

Economists make a distinction between two different kinds of network: 'one-way' and 'two-way' networks. A one-way network is typically a distribution system like terrestrial television or a bank's automatic teller machines (ATMs). The network is used to distribute a service from one node to all the others on the network. However, communication can go only in one direction. In contrast a 'two-way' network is interactive; it is possible for each node to communicate with all the others. Examples of such two-way, interactive networks include mobile phones, the Internet and railways.

For economists, the most important characteristic of networks is that they produce 'network externalities', which means that as the number of goods sold increases, so does their value. This is counter to the usual presumption of economists that as the number of goods increases their value declines. The increase in value can arise in one of two ways. In the case of a two-way network it can occur directly: as the number of nodes attached to the network increases, so does the number of possible connections, and also the value of connection to the network. In the case of a one-way network the increase in value is indirect. The number of goods is the same as the number of nodes. However, economies of scale intervene and reduce the cost to each consumer.[2]

---

1   T. Berners-Lee, *Weaving the Web*, Orion Business Books, 1999, p. 16.
2   N. Economides, 'The Economics of Networks', *International Journal of Industrial Organization*, vol. 14, no. 2, March 1996.

It follows that additional investment in developing a two-way network brings increasing rates of return. These increasing returns can be described by Metcalfe's Law, named after Robert Metcalfe, the inventor of computer networking, who explained that as the number of nodes in a network increases, so the number of possible connections increases by the square of the number of people connected to it.[3]

Metcalfe's Law applies obviously to such two-way networks as railways, telephones and the Internet. It explains their explosive growth compared with such communications systems as radio or television, where the number of connections equals merely the number of people connected to the system. However, as David Reed, a former chief of design at the computer software company Lotus, has pointed out, the Internet may actually involve an even larger number of possible connections. The Internet allows for the easy formation of groups, and this means that the number of possible connections increases not by the square of the number of nodes but by the power – not N^2, but N^N. Thus three people can form three groups of two and one of three. But four people can form eleven groups and five people 26. As the number of people with access to the network increases, the number of possible groups increases explosively. Figure 2 shows how Metcalfe's and Reed's Laws appear to justify the optimists who claim that the ICT revolution must lead to phenomenal rates of economic growth. As the number of nodes increases with the passage of time, so the number of possible connections increases.

To what degree do Metcalfe's and Reed's Laws apply to the

---

3   This is not quite correct – the number of possible connections equals the square of the number of nodes *less* one. This allows for the impossibility of making a connection with oneself.

Figure 2 **Metcalfe's and Reed's Laws**

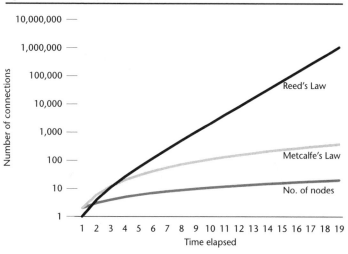

development of railways and the two-way networks of the ICT revolution? First, the laws state only the *maximum* number of connections possible and do not predict the actual number made. Second, while it is clear that Metcalfe's Law can apply to both the railways and the ICT networks, Reed's Law is unlikely to apply to railway networks except to a limited extent. Groups are formed easily on the Internet in the form of chat rooms, business-to-business 'B2B' markets, and retail auction websites amongst others. In the case of railways, the network cannot really be used to form groups except perhaps in the very limited form of group excursions. Figure 3 shows the extent to which the EBRs in their first decades appear to follow Metcalfe's Law with rapid expansion as the system covered the major cities and regions of Britain. The index of passenger journeys is a proxy for the growth in the

Figure 3   **Early British railways and Metcalfe's Law**

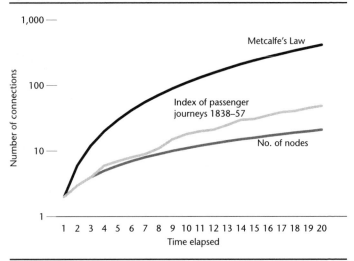

number of connections, and demonstrates how the value of the railway network increased rapidly, yet obviously far less than the maximum suggested by Metcalfe's Law.

The economist Paul Krugman argues that this analysis is too simplistic on another count. He points out, using the analogy of the growth of the US telegraph system, that the first connections are between the largest cities, but once these are linked the next connections can only be to smaller cities. It follows that in the construction of the telegraph network Metcalfe's Law may apply initially, but not as the network becomes more developed. He concludes that because cities varied greatly in size, the network as a whole was not subject to increasing returns.[4] Krugman further

4   P. Krugman, *Networks and Increasing Returns: A Cautionary Tale* [http://web.edu/ krugman/www/metcalfe.htm], December 1999.

explains that the size of cities in the United States is distributed according to a 'rank-size rule', with the second-largest city having a population half that of the largest, and so on. This means that although the initial links in the network will be subject to increasing returns, later links between smaller cities will not. There will be more traffic between the major population centres than there will be between small towns. Krugman calls this effect 'De Long's Law' after the University of California economist, Bradford De Long, who first described it.

Paul Krugman's analysis of the combination of Metcalfe's and De Long's Laws can easily be applied to the development of the EBR network. The first investments in a network will enjoy increasing returns, but later investments will have smaller increases and eventually decreasing returns. The following analysis shows how the laws apply to the development of the EBR network and also to aspects of the ICT revolution.

Metcalfe's and De Long's Laws and the EBRs

The first lines were built between the major cities and the gaps between filled with branch lines once the main lines had been completed. Although in the 1830s and 1840s the English cities and counties did not follow the rank-size rule in terms of their population, it is clear that London has a particular importance compared with other English towns. It would always have been very likely that the most traffic would be between London and the provincial cities.

Table 3 shows that the population of the English cities and counties does not follow the proportionate decline in size suggested by the rank-size rule, but they demonstrate a similar

Table 3 **The population of English cities in 1841 and the 'rank-size' rule**

City	Population ('000s)	% of next largest city	County	Population ('000s)	% of next largest county
London	1,949		London	1,949	
Liverpool	299	15.3	Lancashire	1,667	85.5
Manchester	252	84.3	Yorkshire West Riding	1,195	71.7
Birmingham	202	80.2	Devonshire	533	44.6
Leeds	152	75.2	Staffordshire	509	95.5
Bristol	124	81.6	Kent	448	88.0
Sheffield	111	89.5	Somerset	436	97.3
Plymouth	70	63.1	Gloucestershire	431	98.9
Newcastle-on-Tyne	70	100.0	Norfolk	413	95.8
Hull	67	95.7	Warwickshire	402	97.3
Bradford	67	100.0	Cheshire	396	98.5

Source: B. R. Mitchell, *British Historical Statistics*, Cambridge University Press, 1988, Population and Vital Statistics, Tables 7 & 8, pp. 26ff.

principle at work. Consequently, with London being over six times the size of the next largest city, Liverpool, the first lines built connected London with the largest provincial cities – see Table 4.

Figure 4 shows how in the period up to 1845 railway construction was concentrated on the trunk routes between the main population centres. These included the links between Manchester and Liverpool, London and Birmingham and one between these two railways – the Grand Junction Railway. In addition, links were built between Exeter, Bristol and London, and between the Midlands and the North-east. Lines were also built between London and Cambridge, London and Southampton and London and Brighton. These railways, which connected the major cities, are likely to have enjoyed increasing returns and positive 'network externalities'. As a result, they generated large profits and attracted

Table 4 **Completion dates of major trunk routes**

Route	Date of completion	Railway company
Liverpool to Manchester	1830	Liverpool & Manchester Railway
Liverpool and Birmingham	1837	Grand Junction Railway
London and Birmingham	1838	London & Birmingham Railway
Leeds and Birmingham	1840	North Midland Railway
London and Southampton	1840	London & Southampton Railway
London and Bristol	1841	Great Western Railway
London and Brighton	1841	London & Brighton Railway
Sheffield and Manchester	1845	Sheffield, Ashton-under-Lyme & Manchester Railways

Source: J. Simmons & G. Biddle (eds), *The Oxford Companion to Railway History*, Oxford University Press, 1999.

investors to other increasingly less attractive lines as the most obvious routes were completed. Figure 4 also illustrates how in the later period between 1845 and 1854 railways were constructed between less important centres that tended to be less profitable.

The combination of Metcalfe's and De Long's Laws explains the railway booms of the mid-1830s and mid-1840s and the subsequent decline in railway profitability that so disappointed railway investors. In the first optimistic period, which ended in the mid-1840s, Metcalfe's Law applied, with railway companies exploiting network externalities. In the second period, in the main from the mid-1840s onward, De Long's Law came to predominate as most of the major trunk routes had been established. In addition to the new 'extension' and branch lines being less profitable than the trunk routes, competition also began to develop for the trunk routes between competitive railway companies. For instance, by 1852 there was competition on the trunk route between London and Birmingham between the London & North Western Railway and the Great Western Railway.

Figure 4   De Long's Law applied to the EBRs

The two maps illustrated show the railways completed by 1845 and by 1854. They also show how, as De Long's law predicts, the lines built by 1845 were the trunk routes between the major population centres. In the later period between 1846 and 1854, lines between the less important centres of population were constructed. It is easy to see why the first, pre-1845, lines were the most profitable.

1845

▬▬ **rail lines**

1854

Source: Robert M. Schwartz, 'Railways and Rural Development in England and Wales, 1850–1914', *Frontières, contacts, échanges: Hommages à André Palluel*, edited by Christian Sorrel, Chambéry, 2002: 241–59, page 247. Adapted and reproduced by permission.

The creation and development of a network by private enterprise leads to the construction of the network in two stages, which corresponds to the predominant influence of Metcalfe's Law or De Long's Law. The stages apply to the development of the British railway network in the mid-nineteenth century, but they can equally well apply, with little alteration, to many of the network technologies of the ICT revolution which are being developed under a similar laissez-faire regime.

Competition in network development

But Metcalfe's and De Long's Laws are not the only influences on the development of the EBR network. Competition between companies over the main trunk routes became intense. Thus by 1852 there were competitive routes between London and Birmingham and Nottingham, and Leeds and Edinburgh. There was also competition on the route between Liverpool and Leeds and to Hull. Fifteen years later, in 1867, there were competitive lines between London and Dover, Portsmouth and Exeter, and Manchester and Sheffield. Britain had by far the most competitive railway system of any country, and attempts by companies to reduce competition by amalgamation, leasing or 'working agreements' had only limited success.[5]

As the major companies extended their own systems, so competition began to increase. The major systems came to dominate territories centred on London like slices of pizza. Thus the GWR had to compete to its north with the London & North Western Railway (L&NWR) and to its south with the London & South

---

5   See the entry 'Competition, inter-railway' in Simmons & Biddle, op. cit., p. 101.

Western Railway (L&SWR). In turn the L&SWR faced competition to its east from the London Brighton & South Coast Railway (LB&SCR). It was only in the 1850s and 1860s that railway companies sought to limit competition by price cartels and profit-sharing agreements.

In the 1830s and the early 1840s most railway companies were formed to link two or three cities, and it was only at a later stage in their development that companies came to realise that they could exploit network externalities, following Metcalfe's Law, by amalgamations. But it is interesting that these combinations actually tended to create competition for traffic on the trunk routes between the major population centres. Perhaps the most successful attempt to exploit network externalities was the formation of the L&NWR in 1846.[6] This involved the formation of a single company to control the route between London, Birmingham, Liverpool and Manchester with connections to the north-west of England and the west coast route to Scotland.

The other important example of the process of amalgamation is that of the railway companies of 'Railway King' George Hudson. In a series of dramatic moves, Hudson assembled a system of associated companies that in the early 1840s ran from York to Rugby, where it joined the London and Birmingham Railway (L&BR) (which became part of the L&NWR in 1846), so forming a route from London to York. The system was based on the Midland Railway, which Hudson formed in 1844 by combining three railways centred on Derby.[7] He was far-sighted enough to see that it could

6   The railways combined were the London and Birmingham, the Grand Junction (which included the Liverpool and Manchester) and the Manchester and Birmingham Railways.

7   The railways combined were the North Midland, the Midland Counties and the Birmingham and Derby Junction Railways.

form part of an east coast route between London and Edinburgh. Much of his efforts in the mid-1840s were focused on organising a route from York to Edinburgh, which involved connections between York and the North-east, the Great North of England Railway, and connections between Newcastle and Berwick. In turn, the chain of railways would be linked to Edinburgh by the North British Railway in Scotland. In June 1844, the first train from London arrived in Gateshead and Hudson was determined to protect his monopoly of the east coast route to the North-east and Scotland. The completion of the east coast route to Scotland would compete with the west coast route controlled by the L&NWR.

Unfortunately, Hudson's east coast route to Scotland had two major flaws. First, the route between York and London required the collaboration of the L&BR (later the L&NWR), which were not part of Hudson's system. This meant that Hudson would have to share the proceeds of traffic between Scotland and the North-east and London with the L&NWR. (The expectation that his railways would need to share traffic led Hudson to be an enthusiastic supporter of the Railway Clearing House – see below, p. 74.) The second more serious flaw in Hudson's system was that the route from York to London by way of Derby and the L&NWR was indirect. There is an obvious direct route through Peterborough, Grantham, Retford and Doncaster, which had been proposed as early as 1827.[8] The scheme was revived in the early 1840s under the leadership of George Denison, who was MP for the West Riding of Yorkshire, and was supported by some of Hudson's Whig political opponents. After a lengthy parliamentary campaign, the bill for

8   In road terms, Hudson's route between London and York roughly followed that of the M1. The GNR route was that of the A1.

the London & York, or Great Northern Railway (GNR), as it was later called, was passed in 1846, and the railway was completed in 1849. Not only did the new line compete with Hudson's indirect east coast route to Scotland, but it created conflicts between the Hudson-controlled railways. It was in the interests of the railways in the North-east to collaborate with the GNR, but the latter competed directly with the Midland Railway's route to London through Derby.

Another means of exploiting network externalities was by collaboration. One important example was the formation of the Railway Clearing House (RCH) in 1842, when George Carr Glyn, the chairman of the L&BR (and later of the L&NWR), invited all other railway companies to join a group to resolve mutual problems. Glyn was supported by George Hudson, whose system based on the York & North Midland Railway had no direct link in 1841 between London and York except by a circuitous route using the track of five other railways.

The RCH, which initially excluded the GWR and some other smaller companies, developed procedures for easing through traffic over the system. It made rules for the 'through-booking' of passengers and privately owned horses and carriages. It also apportioned passenger receipts on a per mileage basis and encouraged the application of the same practice to goods.[9] The RCH also provided for the settlement of inter-company debts. It was financed by a £5 per station charge and a levy on receipts. The RCH had much less immediate success in persuading member companies to adopt the same working practices, but from 1847 it

---

9 The procedure for 'through' booking has similarities with the 'packet switching' used to transmit data across the Internet.

tracked the movements of rolling stock on 'foreign' lines and apportioned revenues.

Membership of the RCH was voluntary, but by the 1860s most companies were members as it was strongly in their interests to maximise 'through' traffic. One important reason for the creation of the RCH was the need to compete effectively with the transport companies, such as Pickfords, which had extensive national networks for the carriage of goods by road and canal. Before the formation of the RCH, railway companies were deeply suspicious of goods and passengers that came on to 'their' territory from other railway companies. It was, for example, impossible to make 'through' bookings. A letter writer to *The Times* described how, in trying to send a horse by rail over two systems of two railway companies, he had to send a servant to move the horse from the wagon of one railway to that of another.

The function of the Railway Clearing House parallels the role of the World Wide Web Consortium (or W3C), which sets standards for the software and protocols that make it possible for the Web to maintain its structure as a network that all attached to it can use. In a similar fashion to the RCH, the W3C has a voluntary membership of participants who pay a subscription. The role of the W3C is not to impose a structure or require servers to be 'registered', and in this respect it is the same as the RCH, which never sought to control the British railway network.[10]

Of course, some suppliers of Internet and Web services thought that they could provide a unique service which would be completely under their control with their members only using the Web incidentally. For example, both Compuserve (now part

10   Berners-Lee, op. cit., p. 106.

of AOL) and Microsoft, through the Microsoft Network (MSN), imagined that they could dominate their own networks and their members would have no use for any other. They may also have believed that there was a good chance that they could become the sole supplier. These hopes were vain, and each has the role of an Internet Service Provider that has its own content as well as providing access to the rest of the Web.

Similar illusions may have been shared by the GWR in its refusal, under the guidance of its engineer, Isambard Kingdom Brunel, to adopt the same gauge as the other railways in Great Britain. Much like Microsoft in its MSN guise, Compuserve and AOL, the Great Western directors believed that each regional or provincial railway network would be complete in itself and that there would be no need for compatibility with the national railway system.

Because the railways faced encroachment of other companies into 'their' territories, the directors of railway companies faced a strategic dilemma. If they failed to dominate their territory, the financial consequences could be serious. 'Enemy' branch lines that invaded their territory would divert traffic and profits from their main lines to those of their competitors. On the other hand, if they built defensive branch lines, or gained control of adjacent railways to consolidate control of their territory, they risked massive expense for little reward.[11] A cheaper alternative was to engage in

---

11 It is interesting that contemporary economists in the 1830s, 1840s and 1850s apparently had no understanding of 'network externalities'. But such popular discussion of competition between railway companies used military and diplomatic metaphors to describe network externalities and the 'winner takes all' character of the competition between companies. Thus, the Victorian railway expert and economist Dionysius Lardner did not analyse the issue in his study, *Railway Economy* (New York, 1855).

spirited lobbying (and bribing) of MPs and peers to prevent the passage of necessary authorising legislation. In the mid-1840s, this was frequently unsuccessful, and large companies were faced with expensive and unprofitable defensive operations. By the early 1850s many lines that had been authorised were abandoned, and Carr Glyn put the blame for what had happened on:

> ... those who, in 1845 and 1846, opened the door of the Legislature to projects designed simply for the purpose of competition ... who forced us in defence ... to undertake schemes which otherwise I take upon myself and my colleagues to say would never have entered into our heads.[12]

The private bill procedure made it relatively easy for promoters to obtain authorising acts even for competitive lines. This enthusiasm for competition probably owed much to the opportunities for graft and directorships which came the way of MPs, but there was also a kind of 'market for legislation' which allowed objectors to railway Acts to be bought off or compensated. An objection or counter-petition could raise the cost of obtaining the Act and lead to amendments that met the demands of objectors, and it meant that costs, such as loss of view or amenity, that otherwise would have been borne by third parties were met by the promoters. But objections on the grounds that a proposed new line would increase competition were only occasionally successful. Even the dominating figure of George Hudson could not prevent the passage through Parliament of the bill to authorise the GNR, which

---

12   Quoted in A. D. Gayer, W. W. Rostow and A. J. Schwartz, *The Growth and Fluctuation of the British Economy 1790–1850*, vol. I, Oxford University Press, 1953, p. 439. Reprinted by permission of the Oxford University Press.

took a direct route from London to York in competition with his roundabout route to London from the North.

An interesting example of this type of warfare was the ferocious battle between the directors of the L&SWR and its shareholders over a proposed extension from Dorchester to Exeter. In the early 1850s, the L&SWR was threatened by the GWR's plans to build a broad-gauge railway (i.e. part of the GWR system) from Exeter to Dorchester, deep into the heart of what L&SWR's directors regarded as 'their' territory. To prevent the GWR obtaining a bill for its planned railway the L&SWR directors made a pledge to Parliament that it would build a double line from Dorchester to Exeter and double the existing single line from Southampton to Dorchester. These proposals were strongly opposed by the shareholders of the L&SWR on the grounds that such 'extension' railways usually lost the shareholders money. By some extraordinary skulduggery the directors succeeded in defeating a majority of shareholders. They also managed to convert the pledge, which they did not have the right to give, into a commitment to build a railway between Exeter and Yeovil as part of a 'central route' to Exeter by way of Salisbury. This had also been opposed by the shareholders on the same grounds.

This bizarre story of conflict between the shareholder 'proprietors' and directors was used by Herbert Spencer in his book *Railway Morals and Railway Policy*[13] as an extreme example of the conflicts of interest between railway company directors and shareholders. Herbert Spencer argued that defective corporate governance, to use a modern term, caused the problem. Directors, Spencer argued, used the property of shareholders for their own

---

13   H. Spencer, *Railway Morals and Railway Policy*, Longman, Brown, Green, & Longmans, London, 1855.

interests and those of surveyors, engineers and lawyers in seeking new lines. While this may have been an important motive in the building of many extension lines, it was not the only motive.

The directors of the L&SWR had genuine reason for concern. If the Dorchester to Exeter railway were not built, it would allow the GWR to 'invade' their territory from the north. This would have the effect of reducing the potential size of the L&SWR's territory and the network externalities it could generate. By the same token, it would increase the GWR's territory and the network externalities it could generate. The L&SWR directors feared that a railway company that was significantly smaller than its neighbour would lose traffic on the frontier between the two systems to the larger network. They may also have believed that in the long run economic growth would have made the Dorchester to Exeter railway profitable. It follows that Herbert Spencer and the L&SWR shareholders were not necessarily correct in opposing the extension to Exeter, as an invasion of their company's territory by the GWR might have had a significant long-term effect on the whole L&SWR system.

More generally, the story is important as it explains the motives of railway companies in rapidly building a network of 'extension railways' and branch lines to define and defend their 'territories'. The companies feared that if they did not expand they risked putting themselves at a serious long-term disadvantage to neighbouring and competing railway companies. Temporary losses on such 'extension' railways were better than collapse, or possible absorption, by a more aggressive competitor.

The broad gauge: the GWR's alternative strategy

One of the most important themes in the development of the EBRs was the decision whether to adopt a single gauge (the gap between the lines) for the whole network. This would have allowed traffic to move easily between the different regional networks that were owned by separate companies or groups of companies. For no very good reason the gauge settled on in Great Britain was 4 ft 8½ ins, known as the 'standard' gauge – a different, broader gauge (5 ft 3 ins) was fixed for Ireland. The decision evolved from the fact that carts in north-east England had 4 ft 8½ ins between their wheels. But the advantage of a universal network of networks was resisted until 1892 by the GWR, which adopted the broad gauge of 7 ft ½ in on the advice of its engineer, Isambard Kingdom Brunel, on technical grounds. By the end of the century it had become clear that any technical advantages of the broad gauge were outweighed by the disadvantage of not allowing through traffic from any point on the network to any other.

Railway experts from the nineteenth century to the present day have criticised Brunel and the GWR directors for failing to see that the broad gauge was a mistake from the outset, and that it was an example of the self-indulgence of their engineer. Brunel himself believed that because the GWR and its branches would operate in a discrete territory over which it would have a monopoly, there was no great disadvantage in a 'break of gauge' with the rest of the national system. In 1838, he wrote:

> [The break of gauge] is undoubtedly an inconvenience; it amounts to a prohibition to almost any railway running northward from London, as they must all more or less depend for their supply upon other lines or districts

where railways exist and with which they must hope to be connected. In such cases there is no alternative.

The Great Western Railway, however, broke ground in an entirely new district in which railways were unknown. At present it commands this district, and has already sent forth branches which embrace nearly all that can belong to it; and it will be the fault of the Company if it does not effectually and permanently secure to itself the whole trade of this portion of England with that of South Wales and the south of Ireland ... [14]

What Brunel did not say was that the GWR and 'Great Western interests' planned a comprehensive transport system that would cover the west of England, South Wales and south-western Ireland with an interlocking web of railways and railway companies. It was also planned to extend the network by steamship connections to Waterford in Ireland and to New York.[15] The GWR directors might reasonably have supposed a network of this size to be large enough to support a separate operating gauge that they believed to be technically superior to the standard gauge.[16] While the network was completed successfully in England and Wales, the Irish famine meant that the railways planned by 'Great Western interests' in south-

---

14   Quoted in E. T. MacDermot, *History of the Great Western Railway*, vol. I, 1833–1863, part I, Great Western Railway, 1927, p. 77.

15   The Great Western Steamship Company commissioned the *Great Western* and the *Great Britain* for the route between Bristol and New York.

16   There is still controversy on the question of whether the broad gauge was technically superior to the standard. The wider gauge allowed wagons and engines to have a lower centre of gravity and larger wheels. See T. Bryan, 'The Battle of the Gauges', *Isambard Kingdom Brunel Recent Works*, exhibition catalogue, Design Museum, 2000, pp. 36ff.

west Ireland, based on Waterford, were not completed.[17]

Unlike other railway companies, the GWR was the centre of an association of companies and investors that formed a system unified by the use of the broad gauge. This had the advantage that it allowed for the exploitation of network externalities across the system and made it more difficult for standard-gauge companies to invade broad-gauge territory. Thus the broad gauge gave the GWR and its associated companies a strategic advantage in excluding new entrants from their territory. This advantage may explain the fury with which the broad gauge was opposed by other railway interests, who may have realised that a large, closely linked group of railway companies united geographically and technically would have made their expansion in South Wales and the west of England impossible. In 1844, the government set up a Royal Commission as a result of pressure by Richard Cobden[18] in the House of Commons to attempt to resolve the issue; this reported in 1845.[19] It concluded that 'an equitable means' should be found of compulsorily eliminating the broad gauge. The GWR had little difficulty in resisting this proposal, but the ultimate result was the passage of the Gauge Act of 1846, which required that any new broad-gauge railway required specific clauses in its authorising Act. In a pamphlet attacking the conclusions of the Royal Commission, the Secretary and Manager of the GWR, Charles Saunders, accused its report of threatening monopoly:

---

17 These railways were the Waterford, Wexford, Wicklow and Dublin Railway and the Cork and Waterford Railway, and would have linked Dublin with Waterford and Cork and formed the basis of a railway territory similar to that of the GWR in Wales.

18 Despite being an opponent of monopoly, Cobden, a leading free trade activist, was a strong opponent of the broad gauge.

19 The Royal Commission on Gauges.

> That the question of the 'break of gauge' originated as
> a cloak to a monopoly, or as a means of obtaining and
> holding a control over an immense traffic by a union
> of amalgamated companies, without the possibility of
> competition or interference with such traffic by any
> contending interest or separate interest.[20]

The threat of monopoly was not merely theoretical. In 1846 George Hudson was at the height of his powers, and he controlled a railway network that had grown very rapidly, which linked Newcastle and Bristol and covered well over 1,000 miles of track. Also in 1846, as we have seen, the L&NWR was formed and became one of the GWR's most formidable opponents.

This objection to the Royal Commission's conclusions was listed first with other objections, including a demonstration of the speed and safety of broad-gauge trains compared with standard-gauge trains. The pamphlet also pointed out that the difficulties caused by the break of gauge were much exaggerated in the case of passenger traffic, as even with a universal single gauge passengers would often have to change between lines. In this respect the broad gauge would make little difference. The paper also argued that, in the case of goods traffic, improved technology including containers could be used to ship goods easily across gauge breaks. But the paper also emphasised the importance of the difference in gauge in encouraging competition and emulation:

> That such rivalry and emulation of the two Gauges has
> already acted most powerfully to the improvement of
> both, and to the economical as well as rapid transport of

---

20 *Observations on the Report of the Gauge Commissioners*, quoted in MacDermot, op. cit., vol. I, part I, p. 235.

RAILWAY.COM

Passengers and Merchandise throughout this country, and
it is calculated, if not prohibited, to extend in various ways
the same and even still greater public benefits hereafter.[21]

Why did the broad gauge fail? The most likely explanation is
that the GWR never succeeded in dominating a large enough territory to make the gauge self-sufficient and for the amount of traffic
with standard-gauge railways to remain relatively insignificant.
There were a number of reasons why the GWR's expansion was
limited.

In the first place, the opponents of the broad gauge succeeded
in persuading Parliament to limit extension of the broad gauge.
While this changed very little in legal form, it established that
proposals for new broad-gauge railways were subject to stiff opposition both inside and outside Parliament. Second, the GWR
was outmanoeuvred by its opponents and its expansion limited.
Through a tactical error the GWR failed to gain control of the
Bristol to Birmingham route and apply the broad gauge to it: it
was outbid by the Midland Railway, which was part of George
Hudson's standard-gauge system. Although the company was
compelled to provide a third rail to allow broad-gauge traffic to
Gloucester, it was a major defeat for the GWR. It was also handi-
capped by its inability to develop a broad-gauge route from north
to south in addition to its dominance of the routes to the west of
England and South Wales. The company was unable to extend
broad-gauge lines beyond Salisbury and to Dorchester, and the
L&SWR's determined opposition prevented any further extension of the system in the South. To the north too the GWR was

---

21   MacDermot, op. cit., vol. I, part 1, p. 238.

frustrated. After initial hopes of extending the broad gauge to the Mersey, the GWR had to settle for Wolverhampton. Again it was outmanoeuvred by its opponents. The Grand Junction Railway, which provided a link between Liverpool and the North-west and Birmingham, hoped to bully the L&BR into making a bid for it by offering to collaborate with the GWR and build a broad-gauge line to Birmingham. This would have created an alternative broad-gauge link between London and Birmingham which would have competed with the L&BR. The result was that the L&BR bought the Grand Junction and the GWR and the broad gauge were excluded from Birmingham until eventually they reached the city in 1852. The limitation on new broad-gauge railways following the Gauge Act of 1846 did not prevent the acquisition of standard-gauge railways by the GWR. In 1861, the standard-gauge West Midlands Railway was amalgamated with the GWR, but the break of gauge within the GWR itself meant that many of the advantages of a single network were lost.

Eventually it became clear to the GWR directors that the disadvantages of a 'break in gauge' were significant, and there was a steady introduction of the 'third rail' to allow the running of standard-gauge trains on GWR broad-gauge lines, but not, of course, vice versa. Gradually, as the demand for through traffic increased, the 'third rail' stopgap was abandoned. The South Wales Railway, which was part of the GWR system, was converted to the standard gauge in 1872 following a request from 269 firms to make the change. The broad gauge was only finally replaced throughout the GWR system in 1892.

The result of the competitive environment

Large profits reduced by competition

The result of these processes was that both the major companies (because of competition) and the newer lines (because of the rank-size rule) were not nearly as profitable as had been expected. The completion of the major links between the major cities meant that the high profits up to the mid-1840s did not continue. The dividends of fifteen leading railway companies averaged more than 6 per cent between 1840 and 1846; they then fell to below 3 per cent in 1849/50 before rising to around 5 per cent in the early 1870s. Railway company profits lagged behind as the economy generally recovered from the depression of the 'hungry forties'.

Figure 5 illustrates this decline in railway profitability and shows how the GWR dividend never recovered the peak of 8 per cent reached in 1845 and 1846 in the whole period between 1840 and 1875. Between these years, economic growth was dramatic: real UK GDP (1900 prices) more than doubled from £538 million in 1840 to £1,146 million in 1875, but the GWR and its shareholders benefited little, and only in the early 1870s did the dividend reach 6 per cent.[22] Over this 35-year period, total railway capital climbed from £48 million to £630 million in the UK and mileage increased from 1,498 to 16,658.

The GWR was not alone in finding it difficult to maintain and increase its profits. The inability of even the best-managed railways to increase their profits over the 1840s and 1850s can also be illustrated by the experience of the L&NWR. The company

---

22 B. R. Mitchell, *British Historical Statistics*, Cambridge, 1988, 'National Accounts', Table 6, pp. 837ff. Over the period 1840–75 prices were broadly stable.

Figure 5   **GWR dividends 1840–75**

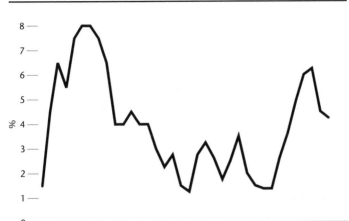

Source: E. T. MacDermot, *History of the Great Western Railway,* GWR, 1927, vol. II, p. 637.

controlled some of the most important routes in the country, linking London, Birmingham, Liverpool and Manchester, and should
have been highly profitable with profits increasing in line with
economic growth as a prime beneficiary of Metcalfe's Law. The
L&NWR was the largest railway company in Britain in the early
1850s with capital of over £30 million (£1.5 billion in approximate
2002 values). In 1851/52 its share of UK passenger revenue was
18.5 per cent, in 1858/59 13.8 per cent, and the equivalent figures
for goods were 18.7 and 16.0 per cent.[23] The L&NWR had to
contend with competition from a number of companies for the

23   From Table 21, 'London & North Western's share in United Kingdom railway
     activity', in T. R. Gourvish, *Mark Huish and the London & North Western Railway,*
     Leicester University Press, 1972, p. 165.

traffic between London and the North-west. In 1846 it enjoyed a monopoly on this route, but soon had to contend with competitive routes controlled by the GNR and the GWR. In addition, a number of small local lines increased pressure on the L&NWR. These included the Shrewsbury & Birmingham, the Shrewsbury & Chester, the North Staffordshire, the South Staffordshire and Manchester, and the Sheffield and Lincolnshire lines. The company had the advantage of having Captain Mark Huish, one of the first professional managers employed by a railway company, as general manager.[24]

But despite the advantages of some of the most important routes in the country, size and highly professional management, the L&NWR failed to make significant increases in its profits. Its net profits for the second half of 1847 were £607,000, and they were exactly the same for the first half of 1860. Over the whole 1847–60 period, profits peaked at £673,000 in 1855 and were as low as £407,000 in 1858 and 1859.[25]

William Galt (an early advocate of railway nationalisation) illustrated the effects of competition by pointing to the reduction in fares between 1844 and 1865:

> From London to Liverpool, twenty years ago, a passenger
> could not make a continuous journey in the same day
> for less than £2 7s 6d., viz by second class on the London
> and Birmingham, and first class by the Grand Junction to
> Liverpool; now, he can go through by first class express for
> £1 12s 6d, or second class £1 5s. Then he required two days

---

24 Gourvish, 1972, op. cit., p. 106.

25 These figures refer to 'Final Balance' of the company after allowance for 'railway renewal costs'. Source: Gourvish, 1972, op. cit., Table 48, p. 274, and Table 56, p. 281.

RAILWAYS AND OTHER NETWORKS

by a third class open carriage, at a cost of £1 7s; now he can
go down twice a day, either morning or afternoon, in an
enclosed carriage for 16s 9d.[26]

One of Galt's motives in proposing the nationalisation of
the railways in the mid-1860s was that the competitive system
was extremely damaging to shareholders. He proposed that the
railway companies should be purchased by the state for large
premiums over their current share prices. Galt was writing some
21 years after the passage of Gladstone's 1844 Railway Act, which
had given the government the right to buy any railway company
whose Act was passed subsequent to the 1844 Act, and which paid
dividends in excess of 10 per cent. This provision of the Act was
not put into effect as, by the time twenty years had elapsed, few
companies were paying dividends of more than 5 per cent. This
option to nationalise is important as it clearly demonstrates the
almost universal belief in the mid-1840s that railways were hugely
profitable investments, that the large returns of the first railways
would be duplicated in the new railways then proposed and that
the high returns would be maintained indefinitely.

Gearing and debt

One of the by-products of competition was that many railway
companies accumulated substantial amounts of debt. In order to
maintain their position in the network, companies raised a large
proportion of the capital they required by issuing debt and by

26 W. Galt, *Railway Reform*, Longman, Green, Longman, Roberts, & Green, 1865,
    p. 123.

guaranteeing dividends on their equity. During the 'large' railway mania of 1844 and 1845, debt appeared to be an attractive way of increasing the return to shareholders, given the highly optimistic assumptions about railway profitability. After the mania, when investors were more sceptical, guarantees on dividends were often required before subscribers would contribute the necessary amounts. By 1847/8, the amounts were very large. The ratio of debt to equity increased to 33.9 per cent of total railway capital in 1844 at the start of the 'large' railway mania before falling to 24.4 per cent by 1847.[27] However, the total of debt plus guaranteed shares as a proportion of equity was just over 50 per cent – illustrating the weak balance sheets of railway companies just as the recession of the late 1840s was starting. Some companies were more severely affected than others and found themselves crippled by debt.

ICT and EBR networks

What lessons can be learned from the competitive development of the British railway network in the early nineteenth century? How can these lessons be related to similar developments in the ICT revolution of the 1990s and 2000s? Despite the British railways of the early nineteenth century involving only one physical network, a number of different parallels can be drawn. These range from the development of mobile phone networks to the incompatibility of the Windows and Apple operating systems and the browser 'war' between Netscape and Internet Explorer.

---

27   H. Scrivenor, *The Railways of the United Kingdom*, Smith, Elder, and Co., 1849.

The mobile phone bubble

The worldwide development of the mobile phone market in the late 1990s has a number of direct parallels with the EBRs. Conventional telephone companies, such as BT and France Telecom, and pure mobile phone companies such as Vodafone, competed to buy the radio spectrum for the new 3G mobile phones from European governments. In addition, they sought to establish, by means of acquisitions, mobile phone networks that included all the major economies of the world. The motive was to exploit network externalities as users would be attracted to a network that extended to a large number of different countries in which 'roaming' would be possible with the same phone. In this respect, the phone companies are in exactly the same position as the EBRs, which, for exactly the same reasons, sought to expand their networks to maximise returns and to prevent their competitors from obtaining a more comprehensive network. Here as elsewhere in any competitive network business, the principle of 'if you're not in, you can't win' applied.

The completion of the first trunk lines between the major cities led to a series of mergers as it became clear that the best way to exploit network externalities was by amalgamation. As we have seen, the formation of the L&NWR and the Hudson mergers were designed to exploit network externalities. The position of a mobile phone company is exactly equivalent. In the same way that George Hudson or Mark Huish of the L&NWR sought to extend their territories to connect major population centres, so the major telecom companies have established subsidiaries in most of the major countries. It was also an important factor in their acquisition of radio spectrum for third-generation mobile telephony ('3G') in the auctions in 2000. The leading mobile phone company, Vodafone,

Table 5 **Vodafone's subsidiaries worldwide in 2001**

Country	Operator	Holding %
US	Verizon	45.0
Mexico	Iusacell	34.5
Belgium	Proximus	25.0
France	SFR	31.9
Portugal	Telecell	50.9
Spain	Airtel	73.8
India	RPG Cellular	29.1
China	HKM	2.2
Switzerland	Mobile Com	25.0
Italy	Omnitel	76.0
Hungary	Vodafone	50.0
Greece	Panafon	55.0
Netherlands	Libertel	70.0
UK	Vodafone	100.0
South Korea	Shinsegi	11.3
New Zealand	Vodafone	100.0
Germany	G2	99.2
Sweden	Europolitan	71.1
Egypt	Click GSM	60.0
Kenya	Safaricom	40.0
Australia	Vodafone	91.0
South Africa	Vodacom	31.5
Japan	J-phone	33.0
Ireland	Eircell	100.0

Source: 'Balancing act of telephone group's debt', *Financial Times*, 2 May 2001.

has subsidiaries in a large number of major economies – see Table 5.

The result was a scramble for licences and assets reminiscent of the railway bubble of 1845, and it left many of the larger companies with large amounts of debt, downgraded credit ratings and share prices reduced to a fraction of their peak values at the height of the boom. The competition for position was exacerbated by the auctions held in 2000 by European governments selling licences for

Table 6   The 3G European footprint of the major telecom companies

Country	Auction date	Licence costs €bn	Major licence holders					
			a	b	c	d	e	f
UK	April 2000	38.5	✓	✓	✓	✓		
Germany	August 2000	50.8	✓	✓	✓	✓	✓	✓
France	July 2001*	9.8 plus	✓		✓			
Italy	October 2000	14.6	✓	✓	✓			
Spain	March 2000	0.5	✓		✓	✓		
Holland	July 2000	2.7	✓	✓	✓	✓	✓	✓

a Vodafone   b Hutchinson Whampoa   c France TC Orange   d British Telecom
e Deutsche Telekom   f KPN   *European Information Society; comparative bidding,
not an auction
Source: *Newsweek*, 28 May 2001, p. 23, © 2001 *Newsweek*. All rights reserved.
Reprinted by permission.

high-speed, third-generation mobile phones. The mobile phone companies felt compelled to participate so that they could obtain positions in the major European countries and maintain a 'European footprint'. They were in exactly the same position as railway companies faced by an incursion into 'their' territory by a competitor. If they did not obtain a licence in each of the major European countries then they would be in an inferior position to companies that did. In a similar way, as we have seen, the directors of the L&SWR insisted on building a line from Dorchester to Exeter against the express wishes of the shareholders to prevent the GWR invading its territory and establishing a stronger competitive position.

Table 6 shows how European governments were able to raise over $100 billion by the sale of their 3G mobile phone licences. The governments concerned behaved in a similar way to the landowners in early Victorian England in seeking as high a price as possible for the land on which railways were to be built. The chief executive of Vodafone, Chris Gent, criticised the European governments for auctioning the 3G licences on the grounds that the high prices achieved would stifle development, in contrast to the situation in Japan, where the government had given away the licences. Railway companies made similar criticisms of the 'greed' of the landowners who bargained aggressively for a high price for their land.

The 3G auctions were better designed than the informal negotiations between landowners and railway companies to agree compensation for the acquisition of land, but the motives of the parties were very much the same in both cases. The Acts that authorised railways gave powers of compulsory purchase to the railway companies, but the price of land was subject to negotiation between the parties. If no agreement could be reached there was a system of arbitration. Initially, landowners sought to extract as high a price for their land and as much compensation for the inconvenience caused as possible. But later, landowners often realised that a railway would bring significant advantages both in terms of convenience and of increasing the value of their land, and from the improved business prospects. Table 6 also shows how the major mobile phone companies have used the 3G auctions to establish strong competitive positions in the major European countries.

But as well as spending some €120 billion on buying themselves Europe-wide 3G licences, the telecom companies were also committed to spending a further €140 billion on construction of the networks. In addition, the top six European telecom companies spent €70 billion on acquisitions as they extended their footprints as broadly as possible.

One consequence of the need to establish a presence in each of the major European countries has been that the mobile phone

Table 7   **Debts of the major European telecom companies (€billion)**

Companies	1999	2000	
Telecom Italia	9	19	
KPN	5	22	
Telephonica	20	27	
BT	14	48	
Deutsche Telekom	39	56	
France Telecom	19	61	

Source: *Connectis*, August 2001, p. 14.

companies have become very heavily indebted. BT accumulated debts of nearly £30 billion, and other companies were in a similar position. The only major exception was Vodafone, which managed to finance its expansion from its internal resources and from making acquisitions by issuing its own highly rated shares rather than by debt. The increase in debt of the other major European telecom companies between 1999 and 2000 is shown in Table 7.

Falling profits: EBRs and telecoms

Like the EBRs, the major telecom companies are suffering from the effects of De Long's Law and competition. In the same way that the large early profits from the trunk railway routes were eroded by competition and the need for EBRs to defend their 'territories' by building branch lines and 'extension' railways, the telecom companies are suffering from the effects of over-expansion. The losses of major telecom companies reported in 2002 appear to represent exactly the same phenomenon as that which affected the EBRs in the late 1840s.

Apple and the broad gauge

The parallel between the GWR's broad gauge and standard gauge and Apple and the PC standard is revealing. Both GWR and Apple adopted a gauge, or operating system, that was incompatible with the 'industry' standard. Both were designed by engineers who believed that their standard offered considerable advantages over that adopted by the railway and computer businesses generally. Both minority standards came to dominate their own particular territory. In the case of GWR and its associated companies, this dominance was geographical – in the west of England and South Wales. In the case of Apple, the dominance has been in the publishing industry.

The degree to which the GWR broad gauge was technically superior to the standard gauge is still debated. According to a recent analysis by Vic Stephens, it seems likely that the broad gauge had genuine *technical* advantages over the standard gauge, but because of its incompatibility with the standard gauge it had eventually to be replaced by the latter.[28] What cannot be disputed, though, is that when introduced in combination with the engines designed by the GWR's locomotive engineer, Daniel Gooch, in the early 1840s, the broad-gauge system proved superior to standard-gauge railways. Not only were the trains much faster but the ride was smoother. According to Stephens, in 1850 it took three hours to travel the 112-mile journey between London and Birmingham and only two hours and 35 minutes to travel the 118 miles between London and Bristol on the GWR. The effect of the superior performance of the GWR and the broad gauge was to stimulate

---

28 V. Stephens, 'A Gauge Too Far or a Gauge Too Late/Early', in E. Kently, A. Hudson and J. Peto, *Isambard Kingdom Brunel Recent Works*, Design Museum, 2000, pp. 53ff.

competition and improvements by the standard-gauge railways. The broad-gauge GWR set a standard that other railways had to match.

A similar pattern can be seen in the competition between the Apple Macintosh system and that of the 'industry standard' PC. The Apple computer company was founded by Steve Jobs and Steve Wozniak in 1976 and its computers were completely incompatible with the IBM PC. In 1981, they launched the Macintosh computer, which was the first to have a Graphical User Interface – the now familiar system of icons and windows. At the time Microsoft was in the process of developing a replacement for the DOS operating system that it had designed for IBM. It appears that the features of the Macintosh operating system were so impressive, compared with the first version of the Windows operating system that Microsoft was then developing, that Bill Gates actually urged his designers to imitate the Macintosh system.[29]

The subsequent history of the competition between Apple and Microsoft replicates that between the GWR and the standard-gauge railways – with the non-standard system forcing its larger standard rival to improve continually to prevent it gaining more than a small market share. Like the GWR, Apple has a devoted group of users who are fiercely partisan in its favour. In the same way the GWR attracted great loyalty, and it had a unique style and company ethos.[30]

---

29 J. Edstrom and M. Eller, *Barbarians Led by Bill Gates*, Henry Holt, 1998, p. 47.
30 It also succeeded in creating one of the greatest brand names in the history of commerce, which survives although the company has not traded for more than half a century.

Browser 'wars' and the EBRs

The experience of railway companies seeking to defend 'their territories' from competition also has lessons that help us understand the browser 'wars' between Microsoft and Netscape. When the World Wide Web was launched in the early 1990s, it only came to dominate the Internet through the release of the Mosaic Web browser in 1992. This made it very easy to access websites because it used a simple 'point and click' method of opening them and moving between them. In turn, Mosaic was replaced by Netscape Navigator in 1995. By this time the popularity of the World Wide Web was increasing dramatically, and Microsoft launched its own Web browser, Internet Explorer, which was included on all new PCs using the Microsoft Windows 95 operating system.

Microsoft's decision was based on its aspiration to control the Internet as it had controlled PC operating systems. In conjunction with Microsoft Network (MSN), Internet Explorer was intended to dominate the World Wide Web and give Microsoft a significant position in an area that it had previously ignored. The result was that, while MSN remained just one network with its own content among many, successive versions of Internet Explorer came to dominate the market for Web browsers. By the early 2000s, Netscape Navigator was failing to match the performance of Internet Explorer, and it became less and less frequently used, leaving the latter as the dominant browser.

Microsoft's strategy to promote Internet Explorer caused considerable controversy and resulted in legal action by the US Department of Justice and nineteen states on the grounds that Microsoft had illegally exploited its monopoly by 'bundling' Internet Explorer with successive versions of the Windows operating system. Much of the lengthy and complex legal proceedings centred on what sanctions should be imposed on Microsoft, and whether, in particular, Internet Explorer should be included on the 'desktop' of computers sold with Windows operating systems.

Microsoft's behaviour has close parallels with that of large British railway companies competing for territory in the 1840s and 1850s. As we have seen, competing companies like the GWR and the L&SWR were faced with the dilemma of invading the 'territory' of the other with unprofitable branch lines for fear that the other company would occupy the same 'territory', hence reducing the first company's network. Microsoft's approach was exactly the same. It was deeply alarmed that it had overlooked the development of the Internet and the World Wide Web and sought to establish its position through the free issue of Internet Explorer. Put in nineteenth-century railway terms, Microsoft was building a branch line into the territory of a competitor which it knew, in the short term, would not be profitable. Microsoft was behaving in the same way as the directors of the L&SWR in building their branch line from Dorchester to Exeter to prevent 'occupation' of the territory by the GWR. Microsoft is in a similar position; the free distribution of its Web browser is an attempt to maintain a position in a particular 'territory'. If it failed to dominate this 'territory', then it risked losing it to a competitor.

4 RAILWAYS AND THE NEW ECONOMY

The EBR and ICT investment booms

One way of assessing the relative importance of the EBR and ICT revolutions to the respective leading economies is to compare the size of investment in the new technologies as a proportion of GDP. In the three years 1846, 1847 and 1848, during and immediately following the 'large' railway mania, investment in the EBRs was respectively 5.6, 6.1 and 4.5 per cent of UK GDP. In 1999, 2000 and 2001, ICT investment was 5.7, 6.6 and 6.4 per cent of US GDP. Both the EBR and ICT revolutions were thought by many contemporary enthusiasts to herald the creation of a 'new economy' which would improve economic performance in terms of productivity and stability. It is therefore interesting that, at its height, investment in EBRs and ICT absorbed nearly identical proportions of the GDP of the leading economies of their time.

What is more, as can be seen from Figure 6, the pattern of investment is similar. From a low start point investment in the new technology increases until, in both cases, it reached 6 per cent of GDP. There are, of course, dissimilarities; EBR investment had a relatively later start date, 1831, only fifteen years from the first of the peak years, 1846, and ICT investment had an earlier start date (off the chart). EBR investment was also volatile with a significant peak in 1838–40 when railway investment

Figure 6   **The EBR and ICT investment booms**

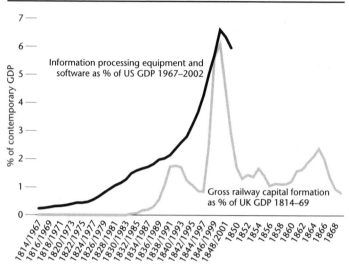

Sources: US Bureau of Economic Analysis, Information Processing Equipment and Software ($bn Chained $, SAAR) BEA Table 5.4, line 9; B. R. Mitchell, 'The Coming of the Railway and United Kingdom Economic Growth', in M. C. Reed (ed.), *Railways in the Victorian Economy*, David & Charles, 1969, 'Gross Expenditure on Railway Capital Formation', p. 19.

was respectively 1.7, 1.8 and 1.7 per cent of GDP in the three years 1838, 1839 and 1840. However, it subsequently declined to 0.8 per cent of GDP in 1844, before beginning the climb that culminated in the investment peak of 1846–8.[1] In contrast, until 2000 ICT investment as a proportion of GDP had increased continuously since the 1960s.

Currently, it is unclear whether, and to what degree, ICT investment will follow the pattern of EBR investment and decline

---

1   As GDP figures before the middle of the last century lack precision, percentages of GDP here and below are only indicative.

sharply after the peak of the investment boom. It appears a strong possibility that ICT investment will follow the pattern of EBR investment as it has in the past and the decline in 2001 is highly suggestive. In the period 1831–69, when much of the British railway system was being constructed, railway investment averaged only 1.6 per cent of GDP compared with the total for all capital formation of 8.4 per cent of GDP – thus railway investment was about 20 per cent of the annual average of all fixed investment.[2] Similarly, one can imagine ICT investment falling back to a much smaller proportion of GDP and of total investment.

Figure 6 also demonstrates how much of railway investment was heavily concentrated in the five years 1845–49, when some 4,000 miles of track were constructed between major centres. In that half-decade, railway capital formation totalled £125.9 million, or just under 30 per cent of the total for the whole period 1831–69. The figure also shows clearly how railway investment also surged in the lesser boom of the 'little' railway mania of the mid-1830s and in the railway boom of the 1860s. In comparative terms, at its peak in 1847, railway investment was equivalent to two-thirds of the value of exports, or twice the maximum value of the Bank of England's bullion reserve in the decade.[3]

Figure 6 demonstrates clearly that EBR and ICT investment share two important characteristics. First, at their peak they represented similar proportions of the GDP of the leading economy of their respective times. Second, EBR and ICT investment is bunched. In the case of the EBR revolution the largest peak by a

---

2   Figures are derived from the same source as Table 9.

3   B. R. Mitchell, 'The Coming of the Railway and United Kingdom Economic Growth', in M. C. Reed (ed.), *Railways in the Victorian Economy*, David & Charles, 1969, p. 18.

wide margin was in 1845–47. So far there has been only one major peak in ICT investment and the large (confidently) anticipated fall in investment.

A nineteenth-century recession in the twenty-first century

The recessions of the 1830s and 1840s

In the latter half of the twentieth century, recessions were often the result of a miscalculation in monetary policy by central banks which resulted in an acceleration of inflation. In turn, this led to central banks increasing interest rates with the intention of stifling inflation, but with the additional consequence of causing an economic crisis and periods of slow or negative growth. Recessions in the last part of the twentieth century were essentially driven by the action of central banks attempting to restrain inflation. In contrast, in the nineteenth century, recessions, and indeed the whole boom-bust sequence, were often caused by an investment cycle that involved the heavy bunching of investment. This is often interpreted by economists as over-investment, or probably more accurately 'mis-investment'.[4]

4   See A. Smithers, *US Profits and a 19th Century Style Recession*, Report No. 160, Smithers & Co., 12 April 2001. Andrew Smithers describes the contrast in the following way: 'The recessions of the post war world have usually been due to central banks tightening credit to prevent a rise in inflation. In these circumstances, prices had usually started to accelerate because output had risen above the trend rate of growth and there was a "negative output gap" … In the 19th century, a more usual cause of economic problems was for the imbalance to be between the growth of output capacity and the potential growth of output. A rise in profits led to an investment boom. The constraint on rising output then became the availability of labour, which was not increasing as fast as the stock of capital. Once this occurred, profits fell and this set off a cycle in which investment declined and unemployment rose' (p. 2).

Figure 7   **Bunching of capital formation, 1831–69**

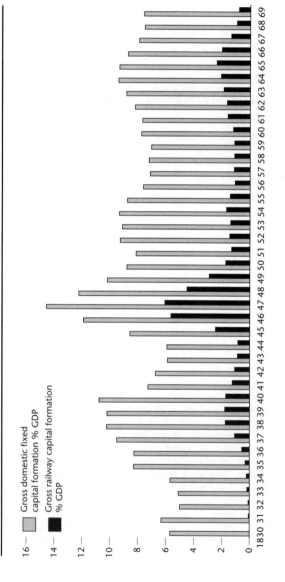

Sources: B. R. Mitchell, *British Historical Statistics*, Cambridge University Press, 1988, 'Gross National Product and National Income', Table 5, pp. 831ff; B. R. Mitchell, 'The Coming of the Railway and United Kingdom Economic Growth', in M. C. Reed (ed.), *Railways in the Victorian Economy*, David & Charles, 1969, 'Gross Expenditure on Railway Capital Formation', p. 19.

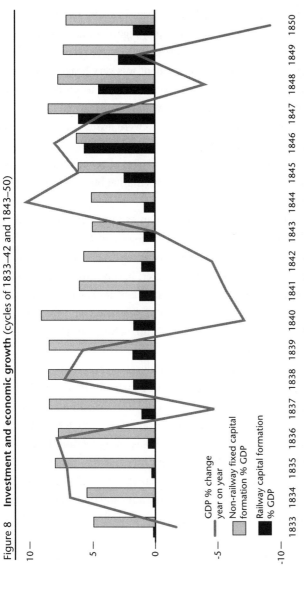

Figure 8 **Investment and economic growth** (cycles of 1833–42 and 1843–50)

GDP % change
year on year

Non-railway fixed capital
formation % GDP

Railway capital formation
% GDP

1833 1834 1835 1836 1837 1838 1839 1840 1841 1842 1843 1844 1845 1846 1847 1848 1849 1850

Sources: GDP: B. R. Mitchell, *British Historical Statistics*, Cambridge University Press, 1988, 'National Accounts', Table 6, pp. 837ff; capital formation: B. R. Mitchell, *British Historical Statistics*, Cambridge University Press, 1988, 'National Accounts', Table 5, pp. 831ff; railway capital formation: B. R. Mitchell, 'The Coming of the Railway and United Kingdom Economic Growth', in M. C. Reed (ed.), *Railways in the Victorian Economy*, David & Charles, 1969, 'Gross Expenditure on Railway Capital Formation', p. 19.

While Figure 7 shows how railway investment was heavily concentrated in the 1830s and 1840s, Figure 8 shows how total investment was similarly concentrated. It can be seen clearly that both aggregate and railway investment was very heavily bunched in the late 1840s. In the mid-1830s there was a lesser but similar bunching of aggregate investment with railway capital formation taking a smaller role. Similarly, there were lesser concentrations of aggregate and railway capital formation in the 1850s and 1860s. It is interesting that the investment booms of the 1830s and 1840s were accompanied by significant stock market bubbles – the 'little' and 'large' railway manias.

The period of the two railway manias can be broken up conveniently into two cycles, that of 1833–42 and that of 1843–50.[5] Both the recessions involved periods of negative economic growth and both had a 'two-headed' character. In other words, both had initial periods of negative growth, 1837 and 1848, which were followed by temporary recoveries, in 1838/9 and 1849; these were then followed by a larger fall in GDP and, in the case of the 1833–42 cycle, longer periods of negative growth.

Figure 8 also shows that while railways were important in the 1833–42 cycle, they were a dominating factor in that of 1843–50. In the first cycle railway investment did not exceed 1.8 per cent of GDP in 1839 compared with non-railway investment of 8.4 per cent in the same year. In contrast, in the 1843–50 cycle railway investment increased sharply from 0.9 per cent of GDP in 1844 to 6.9 per cent of GDP in 1847. Economic historians have maintained that the delay between the authorisation of railways and their construction meant that the railways had a contra-cyclical effect in 1846–8, when

5   This division of the period is that of Gayer et al., op. cit., pp. 242–341.

railway investment was at its peak. However, it failed to prevent the fall in GDP in 1848, although it may have mitigated it.

This contra-cyclical character of railway investment is unlikely to be repeated with ICT investment, which does not involve the same long time lags. The peak of railway authorisations was in 1845, and investment peaked two years later in 1847. It is evident that railway investment was important in both cycles, but especially in the period 1842–50 – as commentators at the time insisted.[6]

Mis-investment in the 1840s and 1990s?

One highly plausible interpretation of the cycle of 1843–50 is that provided by 'Austrian' analysis of the trade cycle. In essence, 'Austrian' economists argue that a theory of the trade cycle must explain why entrepreneurial failure is concentrated. Their explanation is that the information provided to entrepreneurs by the pricing system is subtly corrupted so that they develop their plans on false assumptions and, when these false assumptions become apparent, the bunching of entrepreneurial failure occurs. The misinformation introduced into the system is the result of market interest rates being lower than the 'natural rate' that reflects time preferences. A rate lower than the 'natural rate' indicates that more resources are available for investment than is actually the case. The result is that businesses fail because they lack the complementary factors that would make them successful. These absent complementary factors could include both physical assets and skills. As outlined in Chapter 5, it is clear that many bubble companies, in both the EBR

---

6   Hawke, op. cit., pp. 364ff.

and ICT periods of 'irrational exuberance', were not intrinsically impracticable, but lacked only complementary skills and assets.

EBRs, computers and productivity

The Solow Productivity Paradox

> You can see the computer age everywhere but in the productivity statistics.

ROBERT SOLOW[7]

Prior to the second half of the 1990s, economists were puzzled by the fact that real economic growth had been lower in the period 1966–95 than it had been in the post-war period prior to 1965, despite the steadily increasing use of computer technology. Real US GDP growth in the early 1990s was well below the average annual real GDP growth for the whole period 1948–95. Average annual US economic growth was 4.0 per cent between 1948 and 1965 and 3.1 per cent between 1966 and 1995, but then surged to 4.1 per cent between 1996 and 2000 (see Figure 9).

Productivity statistics told the same story but in a more extreme form. Both US labour and multi-factor productivity remained low over the period from 1974 to 1995 before accelerating sharply. The increase in labour productivity jumped from 1.4 per cent and 1.5 per cent in the periods 1974–90 and 1991–95 respectively to 2.6 per cent in the period 1996–99.

The slow pace of growth prior to 1995, in contrast to earlier

---

7   R. Solow, *New York Review of Books*, July 1987.

Figure 9   **Real US GDP growth, 1966–2000**

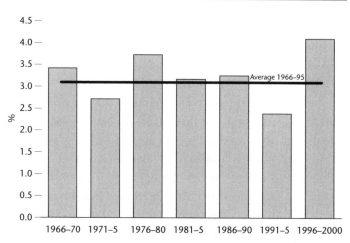

Source: US Bureau of Economic Analysis, NIPA GDP ($bn Chained $, SAAR) BEA Table 1.10, line 1 (1996 prices).

periods, was puzzling in view of the apparent evidence of the increased use of computers in business and everyday life – hence Professor Solow's famous aphorism, coined in 1987. Economists expended much effort in attempting to explain, or to explain away, the slow pace of growth. For example, Professor Robert Gordon argued that the Solow Paradox could be explained by the fact that computer technology was not one of the transforming technologies like electrification or automobiles. Consequently, it was not surprising that the ICT revolution did not have much effect on economic growth or productivity. The acceleration in productivity growth in the period 1996–9 was explained as a typical effect of the late stage of an economic cycle. In other words, he discerned no change in the trend of productivity growth in the late 1990s.[8] Gordon also attributed productivity growth in the period 1996–9 to improvements in the computer industry itself. In contrast, Stephen Oliner and Daniel Sichel explain the paradox by arguing that until the second half of the 1990s computers were not sufficiently in use for them to have any significant effect on growth or productivity.[9]

Another argument much favoured by Federal Reserve Chairman Alan Greenspan is not that the use of computers was insufficient until the second half of the 1990s to affect growth and productivity, but that it takes a long time for the effect of a new technology to diffuse through the economy. Thus, Paul David argues that it took many years for the effect of electricity technology to have an effect on economic growth and productivity. The technology was invented in the 1880s, but it was not until the 1920s that its full effects were felt. The reason for the lag was that businesses only installed the new technology when they would have, in any case, replaced older machinery. One difficulty with this parallel is that, although electricity involves networks, these are only one-way and not the two-way networks of computers (and railways) – see Chapter 3. Another problem is that computer technology has not merely replaced older technology but has allowed the development of completely new processes and activities.

Railways and 'social savings'

In contrast to the analysis of the contribution of the ICT revolution

8   R. J. Gordon, 'Does the "New Economy" Measure Up the Great Inventions of the Past?', *Journal of Economic Perspectives*, 2000.

9   S. D. Oliner and D. E. Sichel, *The Resurgence of Growth in the late 1990s: Is Information Technology the Story?*, Federal Reserve Board, May 2000, Table 2, p. 25.

Table 8   'Social saving' from the railways in 1865

	£m	% of UK GDP £870m*
Passenger traffic	17.5–47.9	2.0–5.5
Total freight	25.5–28.1	2.9–3.2
TOTAL	43.0–76.0	4.9–8.7

*Estimates have been calculated as percentages of UK GDP of £870m – Feinstein's 'compromise' estimate in B. R. Mitchell, *British Historical Statistics*, Cambridge University Press, 1988, 'National Accounts', Table 5A, p. 836.

Source: G. R. Hawke, *Railways and Economic Growth in England and Wales 1840–1870*, Oxford University Press, 1970, p. 188. Reprinted by permission of the Oxford University Press.

to economic growth, the equivalent analysis of the EBR revolution is complicated by the fact that the analysis was mainly undertaken long after the event. As a result economists are forced to use statistics that are incomplete and designed for a different purpose, and derived from secondary sources. It follows that there can be wide divergence in the estimates of the significance of railways to the British economy in the nineteenth century.

In 1970, the economist Gary Hawke attempted to answer the question of the contribution of the EBRs to the Victorian economy by using the concept of 'social savings'.[10] The concept measures the difference in transportation costs in a given year with and hypothetically without railways.[11] Of course, the calculation can never be exact, even if adequate data are available, as it is impossible to assess correctly the numerous counterfactuals that the

10   Hawke, op. cit., pp. 6ff. Hawke's book can be seen as a British version of R. W. Fogel's book, *Railroads and American Economic Growth: Essays in Econometric History* (Johns Hopkins Press, 1964), which analysed the role of the railways in the American economy in the nineteenth century, and together with A. Fishlow's *American Railroads and the Transformation of the Ante-Bellum Economy* (Cambridge, MA, 1965) was the origin of the concept of the 'social saving' as used by Hawke.

11   Ibid.

Table 9   Alternative estimates of 'social saving' from the railways in 1865

	£m	% of UK GDP £870m*
Passenger traffic	4.6–116.7	0.5–13.4
Total freight	12.5–30.6	1.4–3.5
TOTAL	17.1–147.3	1.9–16.8

*Estimates have been calculated as percentages of UK GDP of £870m – Feinstein's 'compromise' estimate in B. R. Mitchell, *British Historical Statistics*, Cambridge University Press, 1988, 'National Accounts', Table 5A, p. 836.
Source: T. R. Gourvish, *The Railways and the British Economy 1830–1914*, Macmillan Press, 1980, pp. 58–9.

estimate requires. Nonetheless, Hawke estimated that the savings, as set out in Table 8, would in all likelihood be closer to the higher estimate than the lower.

The large range in the estimates (£43 million to £76 million) is explained by the use of high or low estimates for the quality of railway passenger transport compared with travel by coach. The higher estimate implies that railway travel for passengers was far more comfortable than for the majority of travellers by coach. But Hawke's estimates have been criticised for the heroic assumptions he had to make to obtain them. Professor T. R. Gourvish shows that by making slightly different and equally realistic assumptions, an even larger range of social savings can be obtained – see Table 9.[12]

Professor Gourvish argues that these alternative estimates should not be accepted as preferable to Hawke's estimates, but that they are indications of the fragility of the latter. He also points to a back-of-the-envelope calculation by the Victorian analyst Dudley Baxter, who estimated in 1866 that in 1865 railways re-

12   Gourvish, 1972, op. cit., pp. 39 and 58–9.

duced the cost of transport to one third of the cost on pre-railway road and by canal.[13] From this he deduces that savings would have been £72 million, or about 8.3 per cent of GDP.

What, then, is a reasonable benchmark figure for the 'social saving' due to railways as a percentage of GDP in 1865? Hawke preferred the higher of his estimates, which ranged between 4.9 and 8.7 per cent of GDP.[14] The midpoint of Gourvish's alternative estimates is 9.4 per cent, and Dudley Baxter's estimate amounted to 8.3 per cent. A reasonable benchmark figure would be 9 per cent of GDP.

It is intriguing that the major differences in estimates should derive from the different assessments of the value to be attributed to the improvement in passenger comfort of travel by rail compared with travel by coach. If one takes Hawke's estimates, as shown in Table 9, then the £30.4 million (3.5 per cent of GDP) range in the values attributed to passenger traffic derives entirely from the way passenger comfort is calculated. In the case of freight traffic the range is far less, only £2.6 million (0.3 per cent of GDP). The contrast is explained by the fact that the estimate of the savings from transport of freight by rail does not involve the valuation issues that make the estimate of the social saving of passenger transport by rail so difficult. Put simply, it is easy to calculate the difference in cost between transporting goods by rail and transporting them by road or canal. On the other hand, similar calculations for passengers are much more difficult because of the subjective element involved. Is, for example, a seat in a railway carriage equivalent to an 'inside' or 'outside' seat on a stagecoach?

13   D. Baxter, 'Railway Expansion and Its Results', *Journal of the Statistical Society*, XXIX (1866), quoted in Gourvish, 1980, op. cit., p. 39.

14   Hawke, op. cit., p. 410.

The issue is important because of the substantial extra cost of an 'inside' seat. This problem of measuring the 'convenience' of railway passenger transport is very similar to the question of whether economic statistics fully capture the advantages of computer use. Thus, the degree to which the extra convenience of using, say, Windows XP rather than Windows NT or 98 can be included in economic statistics is a lively issue for economists, and is in essence little different from the question of how to evaluate the convenience of railway passenger traffic.

Technology 'diffusion' and EBR and ICT productivity

One solution that has been suggested as a means of resolving the 'Solow Productivity Paradox' is that there is a long time lag between the introduction of computer technology and it having a significant effect on economic growth and productivity statistics. As has been noted already, in a series of articles the economist Paul A. David has taken the example of the electricity industry in the USA (and other countries) to argue that it was only in the 1920s that the electricity industry had a significant effect on productivity, although electrification had begun in the 1890s.[15] David explains that, while evidence of the electrical age was abundant at the turn of the century, it took a further two decades for the new industry to have an appreciable effect on productivity.

The explanation for the time lag between the development of the concept of electric power and its effect on growth and productivity is twofold. First, he argues, it took some time for the previous

---

15 P. A. David, 'The Dynamo and the Computer: An Historical Perspective on the Modern Productivity Paradox', *American Economic Review*, May 1990.

factory power systems to wear out and to be replaced by the new electric technology. The slow pace of factory electrification was:

> … attributable to the unprofitability of replacing still serviceable manufacturing plants embodying production technologies adapted to the old regime of mechanical power derived from water and steam.[16]

This meant also that it was the newer industries, such as tobacco, transportation equipment and electrical machinery, having no old technology legacy, which could install the very latest and most efficient electrical plant.

The second major factor leading to the delayed effect of electrification was that it was only in the period 1914–17 that electricity prices fell dramatically relative to the general price level. Then, central generating stations that distributed power to factories came to predominate over power generation at the factory site. The drop in price was also helped by the fall in regulated electricity prices.[17]

The result of the delay in the diffusion of electric power was that in the 1920s there was a marked acceleration in growth and productivity in the US after a period in which growth was sluggish. Thus total factor productivity grew 1.5 per cent per year between 1899 and 1909, 0.8 per cent between 1909 and 1919, and 5.6 per cent between 1919 and 1929. At the same time penetration of electrical drive in factories increased from 24.7 per cent in 1909 to 78.4 per cent in 1929. And David estimates that half the five percentage point acceleration in aggregate total factor productivity

16   Ibid., p. 357.
17   Ibid., p. 356.

Figure 10 **EBR diffusion**

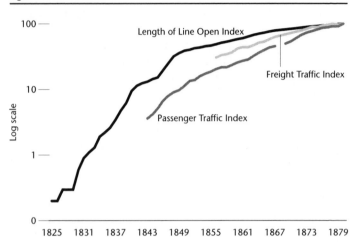

Source: B. R. Mitchell, *International Historical Statistics, Europe, 1750–1993*, 4th ed., Macmillan, 1998, Tables.

in the US manufacturing sector between 1919 and 1929 compared with 1909–19 could be attributed to 'secondary' electric motors installed in factories.[18]

Evidence of the railways is everywhere but in the productivity statistics

This evidence of slow diffusion of the benefits of electricity on growth and productivity is replicated by the development of the EBRs. Indeed, at the time of the 'large' railway mania of 1845, it would have been possible for an informed commentator to have

18 Ibid., p. 359.

uttered a railway version of Solow's aphorism – 'There is evidence of railways everywhere but in the productivity statistics'. As we have seen, the best estimate is that it was only by 1870, 25 years after the major railway investment boom of the mid-1840s, that the social saving due to the railways reached about 9 per cent of GDP, and that between 1849 and 1870 the mileage of lines open tripled while the passenger 'social saving' multiplied six times.[19] It took a long time for the potential of railways to be realised.

Figure 10 shows how it was only gradually that the use of the railway system caught up with its development. The figure shows indices of length of line open and freight traffic with figures for 1880 represented as 100. Data for both passenger and rail traffic is incomplete, but the data is sufficient to show that, in particular, passenger traffic increased significantly well after the opening of new railway mileage.

While the EBRs demonstrate the same delayed effect on growth as electricity, the reasons for the slow diffusion process are different. In the case of the EBRs, the slow diffusion was not the result of businesses waiting until an older technology had worn out before replacing it with railways. Although railways and electricity share the property of being general-purpose technologies (GPTs) (see Chapter 2, p. 37), there are significant differences. No one waited till a canal or stagecoach wore out before building a railway. On the other hand, Paul David identifies other factors in the exploitation of electric power which apply to the diffusion of railway technology. He points out that the introduction of the new technology inevitably involved a learning process and the formation of a cadre of experts familiar with the technology.[20]

19   Hawke, op. cit., Tables 11.02 and 11.07, pp. 48ff and 88ff.
20   David, 1990, op. cit., p. 358.

Because of the differences between railway and electrical technology and the fact that the former is a two-way communications network rather than a one-way distributive system, the learning process is different. With electric power, the uses to which it could be put in manufacturing are well defined. In the case of a communications system, applications are far less limited in scope. The *Oxford Companion to British Railway History*[21] includes descriptions of a number of uses for railways which could never have been imagined when they were being built. Take, for example, the *Companion*'s entry for 'horse-racing'.[22] It explains how the railways came to be used to move horses to distant racecourses and transformed the sport from being the pursuit of a few to a nationally organised popular sport for the many. It took some time for those engaged in horse racing to realise how railways could be used to improve the sport. The process of learning how to use railway transport in new ways could not take place overnight. It involved experiment, trial and error, and required an elapse of time.

The existence of a 'Solow Paradox' in the development both of the EBRs and the application of electricity, and a significant gap between the invention of the new technology and its application in a way that affected economic statistics, suggests that the ICT revolution has gone through a similar process. The surge in US productivity in the late 1990s appears to replicate the surge in productivity in the 1920s as a result of the application of electrical technology and the jump in the social saving due to the EBRs in the 1860s.

The example of the EBRs may be more useful than that of elec-

---

21   Simmons and Biddle, op. cit.

22   Ibid., p. 210.

tricity. Unlike electricity, the EBR and the ICT revolutions involve two-way communication networks and, as a result, they may go through similar processes of experiment and learning. It is easy to imagine users of ICT technology only gradually discovering what the new technology could do by a process of trial, error and serendipity.

Quantifying the effect of new technology

As we have seen, the EBR revolution has caused problems for economic historians who have attempted to estimate the size of its effect on the Victorian economy. The problem does not lie with the railways' function in reducing transport costs. This calculation is fairly easily made. The cost of shipping goods by canal or road is compared with shipping the equivalent goods by rail. But the difficulty arises, as we have seen, in estimating the value of new goods that are qualitatively different from those that existed before, and this is particularly true where the advantages flow directly to individuals.

In calculating the value of railway compared with coach travel, much turns on whether travel by rail was the equivalent of expensive travel 'inside' a coach or cheaper travel 'outside'. Another puzzle for the economic historian is the value he should give to the extra speed of railway travel compared with that by coach.

The electricity revolution appears to be less susceptible to this kind of valuation difficulty than the EBRs. Electricity offered the same kinds of straightforward economies over steam power in manufacturing as did railways over canal or road freight transport. It is simply a matter of calculating the reduced cost of electric power over steam. But even here difficulties in valuation arise. Paul David points out that electric power had advantages in industrial organisation that were much more difficult to quantify. Writing before the Solow Productivity Paradox had been apparently resolved by the growth spurt of 1996–2000, he argued that new commodities involved unmeasured changes in quality, and in the early stages of the development of a new technology there was a bias towards goods and services that were not captured by conventional production or consumption statistics.[23]

David cites the examples of the initial use of electricity for lighting and transport, where it was especially difficult to capture the improvements in economic statistics. He points out that the advantages of using electricity for powering trams included reduced travel and waiting times and greater convenience[24] – the same hard-to-measure advantages that complicated the calculation of the social saving resulting from the introduction of railways. David also points out that the widespread use of electricity as a power source in factories greatly improved working conditions – again an increase in economic welfare not captured in conventional statistics.

Exactly the same problems of measurement appear in the ICT revolution. The Boskin Commission, which reported in 1996,[25] found that the US Consumer Price Index overstated inflation (and consequently understated economic growth) because, amongst other things, it did not make appropriate allowance for changes in the quality of such things as computer technology. If no allowance were made for these qualitative changes, the rate of inflation

23   David, 1989, op. cit., p. 20.

24   Ibid., p. 21.

25   M. J. Boskin et al., *Toward a More Accurate Measure of the Cost of Living,* Final Report to the US Senate Finance Committee, 1996.

would be overstated. While the price of a computer may have remained the same between 1990 and 2000, it was many times more powerful at the end of that period. And the convenience of using Windows XP rather than DOS is palpable in the same way that the extra comfort and speed of travelling by train compared with coach is, and it is also perhaps equally difficult to quantify.

One obvious problem is that new commodities only tend to be included in consumer price indices (CPIs) some time after their introduction and after their price has fallen significantly. The Boskin Commission calculated that the upward bias in inflation attributable to the failure to capture quality changes was 0.6 percentage points per annum in 1995/6.[26] As a result of this criticism, the US CPI now makes some allowance for changes in the quality of goods by the introduction of so-called 'hedonic' adjustments to price indices which attempt to make allowance for improvements in such new commodities.[27]

The difficulty of allowing properly for the qualitative improvements created by new technologies may mean that Solow Productivity Paradoxes may be inevitable when there are technological revolutions. The contributions to economic welfare of the new technologies are difficult to value and their effects on the 'old economy' appear only after a long delay as businesses learn how to exploit them. It follows that economic policy-making may be especially difficult in periods when new technologies are burgeoning.

---

26 R. J. Gordon, *The Boskin Report and Its Aftermath*, NBER Working Paper 7759, June 2000, p. 12.

27 Improvements in computer technology are not alone in being difficult to capture in economic statistics, as improvements in medical treatment create the same problem.

New technology and stability

While it was a commonplace in the 1840s that the EBR revolution would have beneficial effects on the economy, commentators were under no illusion that the new technology would stabilise the economy. For example, the editorial writer in *The Economist Railway Monitor* in October 1845 accepted that the railways would transform the productivity of the economy, but he was also concerned that the surge in railway investment might lead to serious instability.

> However free we are to admit the advantages of railways as a means of investing the accumulation of the country, it is nevertheless a most essential thing that we should not attempt to carry out these improvements faster than the capital of the country will permit ...[28]

The editor was concerned that the railway investment boom was on such a scale as to be unsustainable. He concluded that the excess 'absorption' of capital would cause a balance of payments crisis; the excessive scale of railway investment was resulting in a surge in imports without a commensurate rise in exports leading to the exchanges 'thus being turned against us'. He concluded:

> One of the most certain symptoms that can be shown of an undue absorption of capital going forward in internal investments, is when we see our imports increasing more rapidly than our exports, or when the former are increasing and the latter are diminishing.[29]

---

28 *The Economist Railway Monitor*, 4 October 1845, p. 951.

29 Ibid., p. 953.

In contrast, some economists have argued that the ICT revolution would reduce economic instability. It is suggested that the introduction of the new technology would reduce the non-accelerating inflation rate of unemployment (the NAIRU) as a result of increasing productivity. Increased productivity increases real wages, allowing the economy to be run at a higher level of demand before inflation forces the central bank to increase interest rates to restrain price increases. But the difficulty here is that the effect is only temporary; once the system becomes adapted to the higher rate of growth of productivity, the NAIRU would revert to its previous figure. There is evidence that the benign economic environment of high growth and low unemployment in the USA in the second half of the 1990s reflected the acceleration in productivity growth.[30]

EBRs and inventories

It has been claimed that the ICT revolution will reduce the inventories that companies need to hold because the use of information and computer technology makes possible 'just-in-time' management. Some economists have argued that, as a result of the reduced holdings of inventories, the American economy would be less subject to the cycle of sharp movements in the ratio of inventories to sales, and the economic cycle would be dampened as result. However, according to Professor Martin Baily, there was no indication of inventories playing less of a role in the slowdown in US economic activity in 2001 than they did in previous downturns.[31]

---

30 M. N. Baily, *Macroeconomic Implications of the New Economy*, Jackson Hole Symposium, Federal Reserve Bank of Kansas City, 2001.

31 Baily, op. cit., p. 249.

Evidence since then does not contradict this judgement, with inventories showing considerable volatility in 2001 and 2002.[32]

The EBRs do not appear to have resulted in a nineteenth-century equivalent of 'just-in-time' management. According to Gary Hawke, there is very little evidence that the railways led to a significant decline in inventories. He estimated that inventory adjustments amounted only to between zero and 0.1 per cent of national income in 1865. He cites the fact that no reduction in inventories was mentioned by contemporary commentators and suggests that in 1865 the annual saving on inventories could not have been more than £1 million. Even T. R. Gourvish's higher estimates do not put the figure at more than double Hawke's upper figure. It follows that stock reductions may have amounted to 0.2 per cent of GDP at most.

Hawke also makes the point that while quicker railway transport might have allowed retailers to reduce their stocks, this would have been offset by wholesalers holding increased inventories. He does, though, conclude that the greater speed of railway transport would have made stock control easier. In this respect the experience of the EBRs may have significance for the ICT revolution. Whatever effect computers and information technology may have had on the levels of stocks held, they have certainly made their management easier.

Lessons of the EBR revolution

Does the EBR revolution have any lessons for understanding the economic effects of the ICT revolution? As we have seen, contem-

32 US Department of Commerce: Change in Private Inventories – available on: [http://research.stlouisfed.org/fred2/series/CBI].

poraries were rightly worried that the EBR revolution was likely to destabilise the economy, despite acknowledging the extraordinary effects it was likely to have on economic growth and productivity. The editor of *The Economist Railway Monitor* quoted above had good reason for anxiety. A full-blooded nineteenth-century recession resulted from the railway investment boom of the mid-1840s and the economy showed no increased resilience to the shocks of the repeal of the Corn Laws or the economic instability resulting from the political turmoil of the 1848 revolutions. It is also worth bearing in mind that the electricity revolution and the resulting surge in productivity did not prevent extreme economic instability in the USA in the 1920s and early 1930s.[33]

It may be that the introduction of any new technology on the scale of the EBR and ICT revolutions may increase rather than reduce economic instability. The process of trial and error in developing and exploring the new technology is likely to lead to collective misjudgements and a bunching of entrepreneurial error. As we have seen, the EBR revolution was a major factor in the cycle of the 1840s, but railway investment was also important in the booms of the mid-1830s, the 1860s and, to a lesser extent, the boom of the 1850s.

New network technology: who wins?

One consequence of the competitive development of the EBRs was that the profitability of the railway companies was rapidly eroded by competition. Chapter 3 explained how competition and the

---

33   J. B. DeLong and L. Summers, 'The "New Economy": Background, Historical Perspective, Questions, and Speculations', *Economic Review*, Federal Reserve Bank of Kansas City, fourth quarter 2001, p. 45.

prevalence of the 'if you're not in, you can't win' economics tended to reduce the profits of railway companies, and Chapter 5 shows how these reduced profits were reflected in share prices. Railway companies found themselves forced to build expensive and relatively unprofitable branch lines to defend their 'territory'. If they allowed a competing railway company to invade their territory they risked losing traffic to what could become a superior network with a greater number of nodes. In the long run, they might risk losses and absorption by their larger competitor.

As we have seen, in exactly the same way that railway companies were forced to defend their territories by building extensions and branch lines that inevitably were not very profitable, so Microsoft, for example, has been forced to defend its 'territory' by giving 'Internet Explorer' away free. The same 'winner takes all' economics applies to the ICT revolution as it did to the EBR revolution.

Both the ICT and EBR revolutions intensified competition elsewhere for very much the same reasons. Professors DeLong and Summers point out that, except in those rare cases where it is possible to maintain market power and high margins, the new technology results in increased competition and lower margins and profits. They conclude that the new technology may be the friend of competition.[34]

In the EBR revolution there were very few railway companies that were in the position of being able to maintain such a position of market power and high margins. Parliament's eagerness to authorise competitive lines meant that such lines were the exception.[35]

34 Ibid., p. 43.
35 The relatively isolated and competition-free Stockton & Darlington Railway may have been such a company.

Figure 11 **Net earnings of EBRs and net social returns**

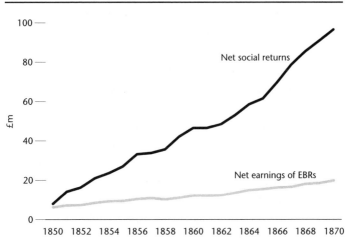

Source: G. R. Hawke, *Railways and Economic Growth in England and Wales*, Oxford University Press, 1970, Table XV.01, cols 2 and 8, p. 406.

In addition, as in the ICT revolution, the EBRs made markets more efficient by intensifying competition between suppliers that previously had been unable to compete because of distance and transport costs.

Social benefits outweigh net earnings

The result of the competition between railway companies was that, although the social return from the EBRs increased nearly twelve times between 1850 and 1870, the net earnings of railway companies increased a little over three times. Figure 11 shows how railway companies were able to capture only a small fraction of the benefits to society as a whole. Given the increased competition that can be expected to result from the ICT revolution, a similar pattern of net earnings of ICT companies being significantly less than the net social returns might be expected.

This conclusion is at variance with the common assumption that unregulated markets worked to the disadvantage of consumers and the main beneficiaries are investors. The evidence of the EBR revolution suggests that it is shareholders who suffer from the 'if you're not in, you can't win' economics of the free enterprise exploitation of networks. It is significant, as we have seen, that William Galt was one of the first proponents of railway nationalisation, partly because he was concerned that competition was damaging the interests of railway company shareholders. Shareholders in ICT companies should not expect a different experience from their railway predecessors.[36]

No case for planning

Although only a small proportion of the benefits of the development of the railways came to shareholders in the EBR companies, there is no evidence to suggest that a better system might have been constructed by central direction, as advocated, for example, by Lord Dalhousie and instituted by him in India. In fact, the evidence is that Britain's highly competitive system created a network that was denser than that of France which, as we have seen (Chapter 3), adopted a highly centralised system for planning and constructing a national railway network. By 1870, Britain had twice as much railway line per person, but its population density was only 64 per cent greater than that of France. Admittedly

36   See below, p. 172.

France's per capita GDP was only 58 per cent of Britain's, so some disparity is to be expected.

Nonetheless, Britain's laissez-faire approach to the construction of its railway network appears, at the very least, to have been no disadvantage compared with the French centralised system in terms of the density of the network.[37] It was claimed in the 1840s, and regularly since then, that the British system was wasteful because it was competitive. But when it is realised that the system was created almost completely without subsidy or assistance from the taxpayer, this criticism falls away. As we have seen, the French system, like that of most other national railway networks in the rest of Europe and North America, involved significant subsidies from the taxpayer. The evidence suggests that the British railway user had the advantage of a denser network without having to pay for it in his role as a taxpayer. What is more, the larger proportion of the total return from railway investment was received by consumers rather than investors.

Lessons for mega-projects

One interesting lesson of the EBR revolution is that construction of the British railway network in the mid-nineteenth century with very little government subsidy or intervention meant that the cost overruns that are so frequent in major twentieth-century projects were minimised. This conclusion has important consequences for the finance of major projects in advanced industrialised countries, as well as for the infrastructure projects that are so important to

---

37   The backwardness of the French railway system hampered the Prussian invaders in the Franco-Prussian war. See M. Howard, *The Franco-Prussian War*, Rupert Hart-Davis, 1962, p. 375.

poor countries. As we have seen (Chapter 1, p. 23), Bent Flyvbjerg and his colleagues have analysed the numerous cases where large projects have suffered vast cost overruns with the initial estimates of total cost proving completely unrealistic.[38] It is interesting that the examples they cite are largely taxpayer-financed projects, rather than those completed by private enterprise. An obvious explanation in the case of government-financed projects is that the taxpayers who will have to pay for any resulting losses are diffuse and have only very indirect control over the terms and enforcement of the development and construction contracts. Those who urge the project on the government in question usually do not risk their own money and have very little to lose.

The experience of the EBRs is highly relevant, not because there were not massive cost overruns, but because the system developed an effective mechanism that prevented the worst excesses of 'appraisal optimism'. By any standard they were very large projects. For example, Brunel's initial estimate of the cost of constructing the GWR was £2.5 million, the equivalent of 0.5 per cent of GDP in 1835, the year the company obtained its authorising Act. A project having a value equal to the same proportion of 2002 GDP would have a value of about £7.5 billion, significantly more than the £5.8 billion (2003 prices) cost of the Channel Tunnel. In the event the total cost was some £6 million, and he was widely criticised at the time for his extravagance. And Brunel was not alone in underestimating the cost of railway construction. Initial estimates for six companies authorised in 1836 were for a total cost of £5.7 million, but by 1843 the companies had spent £11.6 million

---

38 Flyvbjerg et al., op. cit.

on capital account, more than twice the original estimates.[39] It is intriguing that these 100 per cent cost overruns are in the main slightly larger than those listed by Bent Flyvbjerg and his colleagues for twentieth-century mega-projects They cite a study of 258 projects undertaken by Aalborg University which showed that cost overruns ranged between average overruns of 45 per cent for rail, 34 per cent for tunnels and bridges and 20 per cent for road projects.[40]

The threat to profitability of new extension railways and branch lines was of major concern to shareholders. The dispute between the shareholders of the L&SWR and its directors described in Chapter 3 shows how the tension between shareholders and directors made the latter think twice before yielding to pressure from the army of engineers, surveyors, landowners and lawyers who had so much to gain from new construction. Indeed, Herbert Spencer's analysis is remarkably similar to that of Bent Flyvbjerg and his colleagues in explaining appraisal optimism as the result of the self-interest of those promoting the projects. Whether or not this analysis is correct and to what degree, it is clear that a tension between the promoters and the shareholders who supply the capital and carry the risk of loss is the best way of minimising the kind of waste that they rightly deplore. The need to protect shareholders (or 'proprietors', to use the helpful Victorian term)

---

39   The companies were: the Birmingham and Derby Junction, the Birmingham & Gloucester, the Manchester & Leeds, the Midland Counties, the North Midland and the York and North Midland. See the article 'Costing Techniques' in Simmons and Biddle, op. cit., pp. 113ff. On the other hand the Grand Junction Railway between Birmingham and Liverpool, the first trunk line to be built, was within its £1 million budget on completion in 1837. It had the advantage of being an uncomplicated route which posed few engineering problems.

40   Flyvbjerg et al., op. cit., pp. 15ff.

can be seen in the decline in quality of construction between the GWR, built in the late 1830s, and railways built in the late 1850s. By that time shareholders had become highly intolerant of extravagance in railway construction. Indeed, it is worth emphasising that it was only in the earlier major railway projects authorised in the 1830s that the cost overruns were large. Greater expertise and shareholder power had the desired effect. In contrast to the largely state-managed mega-projects of the twentieth century, the EBRs demonstrated an ability to improve the accuracy of their cost estimates. With the government eschewing any form of subsidy, shareholders would not stand for anything less.

If this analysis is correct, then major construction projects such as the Channel Tunnel or high-speed (TGV) railways are best left strictly to private enterprise so that the tension between the shareholders and risk-bearers and those promoting the projects is allowed full play. It implies a sophisticated and unrestrained capital market where projects can compete for the support of capital providers. The important social role of the tension between shareholders is to prevent the waste that appears to be endemic where governments and politicians appraise projects without risking their own money. Such creative tension appears particularly important in Third World countries where capital is limited and waste has more serious consequences.

This conclusion strongly reinforces that of Bent Flyvbjerg and his colleagues: that risk capital has an important role as a means of reducing the cost overruns that have been so characteristic of mega-projects.

5 RAILWAY AND ICT BUBBLES

Investment in the early nineteenth century

One of the most intriguing parallels between the development of the EBRs and ICT is that in both cases much of the capital was raised on the stock exchange and the process was accompanied by wild speculation.

The stock exchange in the 1830s and 1840s

The British stock exchange in the 1830s and 1840s was a far from unsophisticated market. Like the stock exchange today, it had a number of sectors representing important sections of the more modern parts of the economy where capital had been raised by share flotation. In the early nineteenth century, as today, the stock exchange was a dynamic aspect of the economy, where the latest businesses and technologies raised money and where the resulting income streams were valued. As well as being a source of capital for railways, the stock exchange was used to raise funds for mines, gaslight and coke companies, and for the joint stock banks following the Bank Charter Act of 1844. The stock exchange had also been a regular source of capital for canal building – the most advanced communications technology prior to the railways. Table 10 shows the relative importance of the different sectors of the stock

Table 10   **Stock market sectors by paid-up capital, 1824–50**

Sector	1824–7	1827–30	1831–3	1834–50
Canals	37	29	28	16
Docks	17	13	12	9
Insurance companies	21	16	16	9
Waterworks	8	6	6	2
Gaslight and coke companies	4	3	3	2
Mines	13	10	9	9
Railways		23	23	44
Banks			3	9
TOTAL	100	100	100	100

Source: A. D. Gayer, W. W. Rostow & A. J. Schwartz, *The Growth and Fluctuation of the British Economy 1790–1850*, vol. I, Oxford University Press, 1953, p. 364. Reprinted by permission of the Oxford University Press.

exchange by market capitalisation in the period between 1824 and 1850, and illustrates the diversity of industries represented and the rapid expansion of the railway sector.

It is interesting that so many of the sectors are recognisably the same as those trading on the stock exchange today, and that railway shares should have grown to 44 per cent of the paid-up capital of the stock exchange by 1834–50.[1] This rapid increase in the amount of quoted railway capital is comparable with the preponderance of new ICT shares on stock exchanges in 1999 and 2000. It seems that in both eras new communications technology came to dominate the stock market. Table 11 shows the different types of companies and their capital quoted on the London stock exchange in 1843, just before the railway bubble of 1844–6.

---

[1]   The only major companies then quoted which have no obvious modern equivalent were the East India Company and the South Sea Company.

Table 11   **Capital of public companies quoted on the London Stock Exchange,** *circa* **1843**

Banks		
Bank of England	£10.9m	
Bank of Ireland	£2.6m	
Joint stock banks	£32.9m	
		£46.4m
East India Company		£6.0m
South Sea Company		£3.6m
Turnpike trusts		£7.4m
70 Railways		£57.4m
24 Foreign mining companies		£6.4m
81 British mining companies		£4.5m
102 Assurance companies		£26.0m
Canal companies		
59 Canals – main lines	£14.3m	
Branch lines and feeders	£3.5m	
		£17.8m
8 Dock companies		£12.0m
27 Gaslight companies		£4.3m
11 Water companies		£2.5m
5 Bridge companies		£2.1m
4 Literary institutions		£1.0m
72 Shipping companies		
24 Land companies		
5 Asphalt companies		
10 Cemetery companies		About £25.0m
15 Loan companies		
7 Salt companies		
83 Miscellaneous companies		
TOTAL		£222.8m

Source: W. F. Spackman, *Statistical Tables ... of the United Kingdom ... down to the Year 1843,* London, 1843, p. 157, cited in M. C. Reed, *Investment in Railways in Britain, 1820–1844,* Oxford University Press, 1975, p. 46.

The stock exchange was not a peripheral aspect of the British economy. In early 1843, the paid-up capital of quoted companies was around 50 per cent of GDP – a ratio of the same order of magnitude as today.[2] But quoted capital was not limited to the equity and debt of companies. Following the Napoleonic wars, government debt had grown dramatically, and in 1843 was around 180 per cent of GDP.[3] All this suggests that the capital market was flexible, relatively sophisticated and liquid – very similar to today's markets.

One contrast between stock exchange investment in the 1830s and 1840s and that today is that the methods of analysis and valuation were much less sophisticated and the accounts that companies were required to publish gave only minimal detail of the company's affairs. These were easy to manipulate, and it was common for unscrupulous directors, such as George Hudson, to confuse capital and revenue. Companies were more often than not analysed in terms of the dividend as a percentage of the capital. The modern practice of calculating the dividend as a percentage of the market value of the shares was not followed. Valuation techniques, such as the price-earnings ratio, had not been invented.

The stock exchange itself had the basic structure that it retained until 'Big Bang' in 1986. The market was divided between brokers and jobbers. The former acted as agents for their clients in obtaining the best price. Jobbers acted as principals and operated as market makers. The market operated a two-week settlement period, which meant that shares could be paid for after they had been bought. Both of these features of the stock exchange

---

2   In 1843 total paid-up capital of companies quoted on the London Stock Exchange was £222.4 million and GDP (at factor cost) was £459 million. *Source:* Mitchell, 1988, op. cit., Table 5, 'Gross National Product and National Income', pp. 831ff.

3   Mitchell, 1988, op. cit., Table 7, 'Nominal Amount of the Unredeemed Capital of the Public Debt of the UK', pp. 600ff, and Table 5, 'Gross National Product and National Income', pp. 831ff.

increased liquidity, making it easy for investors to buy and sell. The system also evolved the process of 'carry-over', which allowed brokers to defer settlement from account to account. In addition to trading on the London Stock Exchange in the new building in Capel Court, there were active subsidiary markets in the 1840s in Liverpool, Manchester and Leeds.

The stock exchange also allowed trading in options, in other words transactions in the right, but not the obligation to buy or sell shares at specified prices in advance. Option trading was forbidden in 1821, but was allowed after the opening of a rival exchange was threatened.

Putting the railway manias in context: the boom of the 1820s

The speculation in railway shares in the 1830s and 1840s was not a new experience for investors. Prior to the 1820s, there was little interest in shares, and most stock exchange investment was limited largely to government securities, 'Consols', i.e. debt secured on the Consolidated Fund. But as the deflation following the Napoleonic wars came to an end and interest rates fell, there was a surge of company flotations, and interest in the stock market increased. Between 1824 and 1825, 624 companies were formed or projected with a capital of £372 million, but by 1827 only 127 were still in existence, and these had capital of £102 million, of which £15.1 million had been paid up.

Following the government's recognition of the states of South and Central America as independent, a boom developed in loans to the new governments and in shares in Mexican and South American mines. With falling interest rates from British government securities, investors were attracted by the high returns

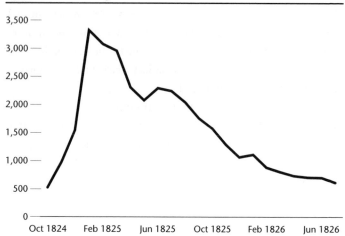

Figure 12 **The mining share bubble, 1824–8**

Source: A. D. Gayer, W. W. Rostow & A. J. Schwartz, *The Growth and Fluctuation of the British Economy 1790–1850*, vol. I, Oxford University Press, 1953, Table 16, p. 374.

offered by the alternatives and by the optimistic prospectuses. Figure 12 shows how mining shares boomed dramatically in the autumn of 1824, but then collapsed in 1825. The mining share bubble of the 1820s was to some degree a rehearsal for the two railway manias, and showed clearly that British investors had a taste for speculation in shares.

The boom in company flotations in the 1820s also showed that Britain had the wherewithal to supply the large amounts of capital that would be required to sustain the railway booms. So enthusiastic were investors in the early 1820s that some of the schemes were reminiscent of the wilder projects of the South Sea Bubble in the early eighteenth century. In 1822, £100,000 (£5 million in approximate 2003 values) was subscribed to a loan to a non-existent country, the kingdom of Poyais.[4] The mining bubble and subsequent railway manias took place at a time when there was a hunger for investment opportunities. This keenness to invest was the result of a stable national debt and a restoration of confidence after the Napoleonic wars. With the yields on government securities falling, there was a natural enthusiasm for higher-yielding, higher-risk investments which was sometimes taken to extremes. Among the companies floated were a small number (by later standards) of railway companies – the small beginnings of what later was to become a flood.

It is worth bearing in mind that this micro railway mania of the 1820s was not the first transport boom. In the 1790s, there had been a boom in canal shares. Between 1791 and 1794, 81 canal Acts were passed in a frenzy of excitement which prefigured the later railway booms. As many canals were planned in 1792 as were then in existence. It was the first time that canal shares were issued by public flotation rather than private subscription, and often issues were subscribed many times over – particularly in the case of the Ellesmere Canal.[5]

Floating companies and raising funds

The boom in company flotations in the 1820s and the subsequent railway manias were possible only because there was an established and convenient method for raising capital for major projects. Although the stock exchange was the market through which shares were traded, the initial raising of capital was often

4   Gayer et al., op. cit., vol I, p. 412.
5   Ibid., p. 412.

done locally. The procedure for launching companies was well established and well understood.

Local businessmen and magnates would form the view that it would be desirable to set up, say, a canal or railway company. They would then make a preliminary engineering survey and announce that a prospectus would be issued. Next a public meeting of interested persons would appoint an investigative committee. If the committee's findings were approved at a second meeting, the company would be formed and a subscription book for initial payments for shares opened. An act of incorporation would be sought from Parliament and engineers, solicitors and bankers would be appointed, together with an organising committee that would manage the project until incorporation, upon which a board of directors would be appointed.

There was no system of specialist venture capital funds or investors, and often members of the organising committee would have to canvass potential local investors. It was often the practice for the proposed company's solicitor to seek capital from a select group of local investors and to advertise in the press. The procedure then was for allotment letters to be issued to subscribers awarding them shares according to the amount of money they subscribed. In turn, those allotted shares would pay the initial deposit, in return for which they would receive either a scrip certificate, or a banker's certificate which could be exchanged for a scrip certificate. The scrip certificate gave the owner the right to the appropriate number of shares once the company was incorporated by its Act of Parliament. On the other hand, the owner of the scrip certificate was bound to pay the additional calls as these became due. Once the company's Act was passed, the scrip certificates were called in and replaced with numbered and sealed certificates issued under the company's authorising Act of Parliament.

This procedure for launching companies encouraged speculation. If the shares were issued partly paid, as was usually the case, it was possible for an initial subscriber to pay, say, 10 per cent of the face value of the shares then, if the market value of the shares went to a 10 per cent premium, the initial subscriber would show a 100 per cent profit. However, there was financial logic to the system. Because railway companies usually needed to raise large amounts of capital to construct and equip the lines, it was natural for directors to issue partly paid shares and to call the unpaid-up amounts as funds were required to pay the contractors as the work progressed.

Another feature of the process of promoting and floating railway companies was that so much depended on success or failure in obtaining parliamentary approval. There might be several companies seeking routes between the same cities with only one being likely to obtain approval. Consequently, there were opportunities for speculation in the scrip or bankers' certificates even before parliamentary approval had been gained or the company formed. Trading in allotment letters took place in the fringe market to the stock exchange – on what later was to be known as the 'kerb'. Companies attempted to prevent trading in their 'light' paper, but there was little they could do to prevent it. Often the motive was to ensure that the subscription lists included investors from the areas on the route of the proposed line. It was thought that a proposal which had strong local support would be more likely to obtain parliamentary approval than one which did not. There was even a 'black list' of subscribers who were known to take up shares with a view to a quick, profitable resale. In the case of the London

& York Railway Bill of 1845, fictitious and fraudulent subscriptions were enough to get the bill rejected, but only for a year. These features of the market for new issues were very similar to the processes of 'stagging' and 'grey-market' dealing that continue today in partly paid share issues.

Little use was made of underwriters or issuing houses, but some railway companies made use of agents, such as banks, solicitors and stockbrokers, to check subscribers, although in fact some must have been used to encourage as well as to check for malpractice. Sometimes the agents were paid for the shares they placed, but they did not take the shares on to their own books and operate as underwriters. Even with the best schemes it was sometimes difficult to marshal enough support. In January 1835 Charles Saunders, secretary of the GWR, described the depressing business as follows:

> The last week has produced about 450 Shares, and I feel now quite sure that we will effectually complete our List of Subscription in time for Parliament. It is however sad harassing work that I have encountered in calling upon and pressing perfect strangers to contribute.[6]

However desirable it might be to have long-term shareholders, it was in practice impossible, because becoming an initial subscriber to a railway company that might not obtain its Act was not a sensible strategy for someone who wanted a secure income from a successful business. An article in the *Scottish Railway Gazette* of 1845 made the point:

> Experience, and recent experience in particular, is quite

---

6   MacDermot, op. cit., vol. I, part I, p. 21.

enough to discourage the individual who wants an investment from becoming an original subscriber. The best lines may be rejected; at any rate, they have no certainty of success, and a man must keep his money lying idle until such time as an act of Parliament is obtained. What is the position of an original subscriber? He signs a partnership deed, by which he runs the chance of losing every sixpence of his deposit on account of the heavy expenses of an unsuccessful parliamentary contest, while there is no certain time when the calls may possibly be made. He is therefore willing to pay a premium to get into a concern free from these contingencies, where he is secured by an act of Parliament as to his responsibilities, where his capital will be regularly brought into play and where he has the prospect of a return for his money. It is clear, also, that the original party, who has borne the brunt, is entitled to the advantage of a premium.[7]

In seeking an authorising Act of Parliament putative railway companies had to follow the rules that had been established for canal companies. These included requirements that before the bill could be heard notices had to be circulated in affected counties and a list of the attitudes of the landowners and occupiers categorised as 'assent', 'dissent' or 'neuter' had to be presented at the Private Bill Office. Maps had to be prepared at a scale of not less than three inches to the mile. Most important, before the bill could be read a second time, half the proposed share capital of the company had to be accounted for under a contract that bound subscribers to pay calls as they arose. In 1837, the standing orders were revised and more severe requirements imposed. The new rules required 10 per

---

7   Quoted in M. C. Reed, *Investment in Railways in Britain, 1820–1844*, OUP, 1975, p. 98. Reprinted by permission of the Press.

cent of the proposed share capital to be deposited with the Bank of England or invested in a trust of government securities before the bill could be introduced. The intention of the change was to ensure that subscribers were not men of straw and had some financial commitment to the company. As we shall see, the changes did little to reduce the speculative fever. Indeed, given the character of the risks of railway investment, it was probably both impossible and undesirable to prevent speculators making the initial investment in what was inevitably a high-risk, high-reward 'investment'. It was also the case that the requirements of the rule, which applied from 1838, could be avoided by borrowing the deposit.

Once the bill had been introduced into Parliament, the promoters faced an expensive, lengthy and in some cases probably corrupt 'beauty contest' before the Act was passed and the franchise awarded.

The two EBR bubbles

Figure 13 shows both the 'little' railway mania of 1835–7 and the 'large' railway mania of 1844–6 in terms of an index of railway shares and of the amounts of railway capital authorised by Parliament. The figure shows how the two manias were clearly separated and how in both cases surging share prices were accompanied by Parliament authorising vast amounts of railway investment. It is worth considering the sheer size of the boom in flotations. Total railway capital authorised by Parliament in 1846 reached £132 million, a figure equivalent to 22.7 per cent of UK GDP of around £580 million.[8] As such it can be taken as a better guide to the degree of

---

8   Mitchell, 1988, op. cit., 'National Accounts', Table 5, p. 831, and Gayer et al., op. cit., vol. I, p. 316.

Figure 13 **The British railway manias of the early nineteenth century**

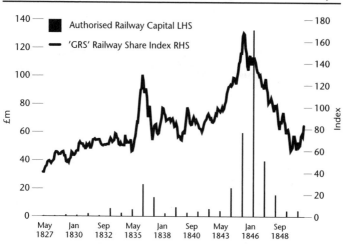

Sources: Authorised railway capital: A.D. Gayer, W. W. Rostow and A. J. Schwartz, *The Growth and Fluctuation of the British Economy 1790–1850*, vol. I, Oxford University Press, 1953, p. 437; share prices: see Annex to Chapter 5.

stock market volatility than the share price index, which is limited to the shares of the major companies.[9] The index was constructed after the event, includes only the shares of the leading railway companies and does not recognise the large premiums paid for railway shares, including those that were never authorised by Parliament.

An important feature of the two railway manias was that the movements in the railway share index were generally in the same direction as those in the all sectors share index. Figure 14 plots the GRS Railway Share Index and the GRS All Sectors Index on a

9   See the Annex at the end of this chapter for details of the share price indices used.

Figure 14 **Railway shares and all sector indices compared, 1827–50**

Source: See Annex to Chapter 5.

logarithmic scale. It can be seen that over the period covering the manias, 1827–50, the GRS Railway Share Index was more volatile than the GRS All Sectors Index, and that it outperformed the latter over the whole period.

The 'little' railway mania, 1834–7

> … there is at present a great madness abroad in regard to rail roads … it is going too fast and will inevitably lead to disastrous results.
>
> JOSHUA BATES,
>
> PARTNER IN BARING BROTHERS [10]

The 'little' railway mania had its origin in the 'Rainhill Trials' of

---

10   David Kynaston, *The City of London, A World of Its Own 1815–1890*, vol. I, Chatto & Windus, 1994, p. 103. Extract used by permission of the Random House Group Limited.

1829, which demonstrated the success of railway locomotives (i.e. mobile rather than stationary engines). In turn, this led to the use of locomotives on the Manchester & Liverpool Railway, which began its hugely profitable operations in September 1830. The world's first 'inter-city' railway connected the second- and third-largest cities in the country after London, and was the highly profitable first link between major centres in the future national network.

The success of the business was such that the company was able to pay a 10 per cent dividend. Together with the similar profitability of the S&DR, it became clear to investors that railways could produce profits considerably in excess of those available elsewhere. By comparison, the risk-free return from Consols, the most widely owned gilt-edged security of the time, was around 3.3 per cent in 1834 before the boom got under way. The 10 per cent dividend represented the yield that could be obtained by the initial investors and not by those who bought in the secondary market if the shares went to a premium. This led to a great enthusiasm for railway shares and new issues. The mania was fuelled by a steady fall in interest rates producing a demand for higher-yielding investments. Figure 15 shows how the mania developed and was cut short by an increase in Bank Rate (see below).

The boom in railway shares began in 1835 with the GRS Railway Share Index at around 60 in May 1835, and culminated a year later with the index at around 130 before it fell back to under 80 in April 1837. The boom centred around the authorisation of major trunk routes. For example, the L&BR and Grand Junction Railway were both authorised in 1833 and were completed, section by section, in 1837 and 1838. The GWR was authorised in 1835 and completed in 1841. As we have seen, investors were greatly impressed by the

Figure 15 **The 'little' railway mania, 1834–7**

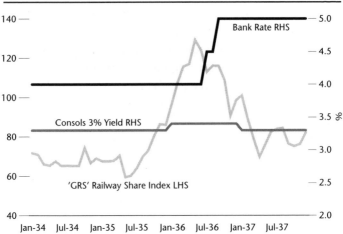

Source: Interest rates: B. R. Mitchell, *British Historical Statistics*, Cambridge University Press, 1988, 'Financial Institutions', Tables 13 and 14, pp. 678ff; share prices: see Annex to Chapter 5.

high dividends paid by original trunk route railways, the S&DR and the L&MR, and believed that other long-distance routes could be equally profitable. The boom was brought to an end by a financial crisis in the USA which led to high interest rates in Britain and a rise in the Bank Rate in August. As in the 'large' railway mania of the 1840s, railway construction continued for some time after the stock market bubble burst. It is significant that the 'little' railway mania is thought by economic historians to have been only a subsidiary cause of the subsequent recession.

The 'large' railway mania, 1844–6

... 'I'm sick and tired of the Three per Cents;

And don't get enough by my paltry rents:'
So he got hooked by the Railway 'gents'

PUNCH, 1845

Like the 'little' railway mania, the 'large' was preceded by a period
of low interest rates and prosperity. Sir John Clapham, referring
to George Hudson, the Railway King whose deals were to be such
a feature of the boom, described business conditions in the mid-
1840s in the following way:

> By that time [the spring of 1844] capital and opportunity
> were lying ready, amply ready to his hand: he [George
> Hudson] and all the smaller, and all the sounder railway
> strategists could plan on what scale they pleased. Since the
> excellent harvest of 1842 wheat prices had been reasonable.
> Peel was cutting duties on imported food stuffs. The
> poorest consumer had a little more to spend and every
> kind of business profited. The market rate of discount had
> never stood so long under $2^{1}/_{2}$ per cent as it did in 1843–4.
> There was no difficulty in converting the outstanding
> £250,000,000 of $3^{1}/_{2}$ per cents into $3^{1}/_{2}$ per cents in 1844;
> because in that year the 3 per cents touched par for the first
> time since the Seven Years' War. At the very beginning of
> 1845 the new $3^{1}/_{2}$ per cents were already well above par.[11]

As in the 'little' railway mania, the most important cause of the
boom was the highly attractive returns from railway shares compared with the relatively low yields available in the bond market.
For example, the GWR's dividend steadily increased as the boom
progressed and long-term interest rates fell – see Table 12. It is

11   J. H. Clapham, *An Economic History of Modern Britain, The Early Railway Age
     1820–1850*, Cambridge University Press, 1950, p. 391. The Seven Years War ended
     in 1762.

Table 12   **Rising railway dividends and falling gilt yields, 1840–6**

	GWR dividend %	Consols yield %	Difference %
1840	1.5	3.4	-1.9
1841	4.5	3.4	0.9
1842	6.5	3.3	3.2
1843	5.5	3.2	2.3
1844	7.5	3.0	4.5
1845	8.0	3.1	4.9
1846	8.0	3.1	4.9

Sources: E. T. MacDermot, *History of the Great Western Railway*, vol. II, GWR, 1927, p. 637; B. R. Mitchell, *British Historical Statistics*, Cambridge University Press, 1988, 'Financial Institutions', Table 13, p. 678.

scarcely surprising that the enthusiasm of investors was excited by the prospect.

The relationship between falling interest rates and the boom in share prices is evident in Figure 16. The index of railway shares was around 200 in mid-1841, but then climbed steadily to a peak of over 400 in mid-1845 (index rebased to 100 in May 1827). Bank Rate fell from 4 per cent to 3 per cent in September 1844 and then to 2.5 per cent in March 1845. The result was a surge of frantic speculation in both established companies whose main trunk routes had been completed and those which were beginning to report large profits and to pay high dividends. GWR shares (par £100, £75 paid) were £107 in February 1844, then climbed to £130 in July 1844 and reached £150 in December 1844. In 1845, the pace of increase accelerated – the shares (now £80 paid) reached £180 in March, before reaching a peak of around £217 in July.

The boom was marked by trading in the shares of new bubble railway companies which closely resembled the dot-com bubble of 1999–2000 – see below. But there was also a very large amount of investment in railways which to a considerable extent filled in

Figure 16 **The 'large' railway mania, 1841–7**

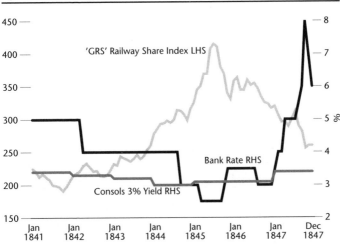

Sources: Interest rates: B. R. Mitchell, *British Historical Statistics*, Cambridge University Press, 1988, 'Financial Institutions', Tables 13 and 14, pp. 678ff; share prices: see Annex to Chapter 5.

the gaps between the trunk routes that had been authorised in the 'little' railway mania discussed above. Many were extensions and branch lines which were built by large companies to defend their territories and which were to result in the competition and reduced profits analysed in Chapter 3.

There was a significant time lag between a railway being proposed and the line being opened. The delay was caused by the long process of parliamentary authorisation and the time needed for construction. Thus Table 13 shows how the peak of completed railway construction of 1,400 miles in 1848 followed the high point of capital spending authorised, £132.6 million in 1846, by two years. As we shall see, the delay had important consequences in bringing the boom to an end.

Table 13 **Railway shares and railway development in the 'large' railway mania, 1842–9**

Year	New	Extensions & completion of existing lines	Total	Capital authorised £m*	Mileage opened: annually†	Mileage opened: annually† (cumulative)
		— Authorising Acts* —				
1842	4	18	22	5.3		1,939
1843	5	19	24	3.9	105	2,044
1844	26	22	48	20.5	144	2,148
1845	76	44	120	59.5	293	2,441
1846	225	45	270	132.6	595	3,036
1847	115	75	190	39.5	909	3,945
1848	28	57	85	15.3	1,400	5,345
1849	–	34	34	3.9	687	6,032

Sources: *A. D. Gayer, W. W. Rostow & A. J. Schwartz, *The Growth and Fluctuation of the British Economy 1790–1850*, vol. I, Oxford University Press, 1953, p. 316. Reprinted by permission of the Oxford University Press. †B. R. Mitchell, *British Historical Statistics*, Cambridge University Press, 1988, 'Transport and Communications', Table 5, p. 541.

The boom turned into a stock market bubble proper in 1845. The mania of subscribing for shares in new railways was described by the contemporary historian John Francis as follows:

> It penetrated every class; it permeated every household; and all yielded to temptation. Men who went to church as devoutly as to their counting-houses – men whose word had ever been as good as their bond – joined the pursuit. They entered the whirlpool, and were carried away by the vortex. They first cautiously wrote for shares in the names of their children, and sold the letters which, while it consoled them for present turpitude, tempted them to fresh sin.[12]

The stock market as a whole peaked in June and railway shares

12 Francis, op. cit., vol. II, p. 145.

in July. Share prices then fell back, with railway shares falling by 13.8 per cent and shares generally by 20.3 per cent in December. There was panic when the Bank Rate was increased from 2.5 per cent to 3 per cent in October and then to 3.5 per cent in November, with many of the premiums on bubble railway companies being converted into discounts. However, the drop in blue chip company shares was less than the drop in the more speculative companies.[13] The increase in the Bank Rate was the consequence of a money market squeeze as a result of the need to meet calls on railway shares. Although the Bank Rate fell in 1846, the squeeze was renewed when it rose to 8 per cent in October 1847. In addition to calls on railway shares, the money market tightening was exacerbated by a surge in imports as a result of the abolition of the Corn Laws in 1846 and the resulting strong demand for foreign grain. Anxiety had been increased by the Bank Charter Act of 1844, which it was thought would lead to highly restrictive monetary policy and very high interest rates in a crisis. In the event, the restriction was not as severe as expected and the Bank Charter Act was suspended.

It is significant that the crisis was caused largely by an increasing fear that the commitments of shareholders to pay calls on their shares was way beyond their collective resources, and that this posed a serious threat to economic stability. The result of the flood of authorisations, no less than £132.6 million in 1846 (see Table 13), was continuous pressure on share prices as shareholders were forced to sell shares to raise cash to pay calls. The weakness in the

13 Thus Charlotte Brontë, who with her sisters had invested in what was then perceived to be the blue chip York and North Midland Railway, wrote to her former headmistress, Miss Wooler, in January 1846 explaining that their investment had not been affected by the panic.

price of railway shares culminated in 1849 when details of George Hudson's frauds emerged. The GRS Railway Share Index (rebased to 100 in May 1827) reached a low point of 149 in October 1849 compared with 415 at its high point in July 1845. Of the 8,500 miles authorised in 1845, 1846 and 1847, some 1,500 miles were abandoned by their promoters under special legislation passed in 1850.

'News flow' and 'deal flow'

The 1844–6 bubble did not involve the launch of the important trunk railways between the major cities. These had been built in the main during and after the 'little' railway mania. The 1844–6 boom was marked by two different types of 'news flow'. First, there were two spectacular amalgamations – the formation of the Midland Railway in 1844 and the L&NWR in 1846 brought about respectively by George Hudson and Captain Mark Huish. The companies were vast. The Midland Railway, for example, had an equity market capitalisation of £20 million (£1 billion in approximate 2002 values) in October 1845 – see Table 15 below. These were deals of equivalent importance to the takeover of AOL by Time Warner in 2000.

The second type of 'news flow' was in the launch of bubble railways, very similar to the dot-com bubble companies of 1999 and 2000. These are discussed further below, but in the majority of cases they were not trunk lines between major centres but lines between smaller towns and cities, for example between Cambridge and Oxford – see Table 14 below. Some proposals were for duplicate trunk routes.

A major factor in the 1844–6 boom was the 'deal flow' created by George Hudson, who expanded from the York and North Mid-

Table 14   **George Hudson's 'deal flow', 1842–6**

Date	Deal	Notes
1842	Takes over North Midland Railway	Line from Derby to Leeds linked to York by the York & North Midland
1843	Negotiations to form Midland Railway	
1844	Completes amalgamation of Midland Railway	Union of the North Midland, Derby and Birmingham Junction and Midland Counties Railways
1844	Conversion of lease of Leeds & Selby to purchase by York & North Midland	6 per cent dividend on £30 of capital not to be called for 18 months
1844	Completion of Newcastle & Darlington Junction	Completion of another section of the north–south link.
1845	Launch of Newcastle and Berwick Railway	Link to Scotland
1845	Buys Great North of England Railway	Link from York to Darlington
1845	Leases Bristol & Gloucester and Birmingham & Gloucester	Extends system from Birmingham to Bristol
1845	Becomes chairman of Eastern Counties Railway	Move into East Anglia

Source: R. S. Lambert, *The Railway King*, George Allen & Unwin, 1934.

land Railway to control a conglomerate that spread from Bristol to Newcastle with an indirect route to London and an (isolated) offshoot in East Anglia. Table 14 lists this 'deal flow', which kept investors enthralled throughout the mid-1840s.[14] Hudson was

14   Hudson's nemesis came in 1849 when he was exposed for WorldCom-like accounting frauds; see Chapter 2.

attempting to control a north–south route based on York as close to London and Edinburgh as possible. His main problem, as we saw in Chapter 3, was that his railways had no direct access to London and had to use the L&NWR's line from south of Birmingham to Euston. His other difficulty was the threat of a direct (and shorter) route from London to York by way of Peterborough. Despite his best efforts, the GNR was authorised in 1846 and completed in 1849.

The railway share market in October 1845

In October 1845, at the height of the boom, *The Economist* published the first edition of its *Railway Monitor*, which was a nine-page supplement to the weekly magazine. The supplement, published on Saturday, 4 October, included a review of the previous week's trading in railway shares and listed all quoted railway shares with their closing prices (if any) for the previous six trading days on the stock exchanges of London, Liverpool, Manchester and Leeds. Also shown were the miles of line authorised and completed and the number and the nominal amount of shares (i.e. the par value, perhaps £20 or £100) and the amount paid up.

At that time, GWR shares were paying a dividend of 8 per cent and yielding 4.9 per cent, although in the case of the £100 shares this did allow for the additional £20 that was due to be called. During 1845, the price of GWR £100 shares had varied between around £140 at the beginning of the year before reaching a peak of over £200 in July. The premium (of the share price compared with the calls paid) also reached 170 per cent in the same month. The GWR was capitalised at £8 million (equivalent to £400 million in approximate 2002 values), which compared with capitalisations

Table 15   **Railway company equity market capitalisations (market cap.)**

Company	Market cap.	Company	Market cap.
Midland Railway	£20,520,000	Manchester & Birmingham	£2,730,000
London & Birmingham	£12,407,624	London & Brighton	£2,496,076
Great Western Railway	£8,066,500	South Eastern	£1,876,000
Newcastle & Carlisle	£3,390,000	Great North of England	£1,841,730
London & South Western	£3,256,200	Newcastle & Darlington Junction	£1,420,000
Liverpool & Manchester	£3,155,305	Edinburgh & Glasgow	£1,350,000
Grand Junction	£3,058,491	Bristol & Exeter	£1,335,000
Manchester & Leeds	£2,912,157		

Source: *Economist Railway Monitor.*

that ranged between £20 million and £1.3 million for the top fifteen companies. Table 15 shows the equity market capitalisations of some of the leading companies.

The total equity market capitalisation of all quoted railway shares amounted to some £100 million, but this is probably an underestimate of total equity market capitalisation as a large number of companies have share quotations but no indication of the number of shares in issue. In many cases this was because parliamentary authority had not been obtained and dealing was done entirely in 'scrips'. In other cases, *The Economist* may not have had comprehensive information. But taking all these into account, it seems a reasonable estimate that the total value of all railway shares may have been as much as £150 million, or about 30 per cent of 1845 GDP. Such a figure compares with the proportion of GDP of ICT share values in the USA in March 1999, the peak of the bubble, of 50 per cent.[15]

In terms of valuations, it appears that many of the established railway companies were conservatively valued by the standard of the ICT bubble in 1999 and 2000. However, there were numerous companies whose shares traded at very large premiums to the amount called (if any), which had no lines built or even authorised and thus had infinite price-earnings ratios like the dot-coms. On the other hand, the Grand Junction Railway, for example, which was a 'blue chip' company that in 1846 was to form part of the L&NWR, had a price-earnings ratio, based on past earnings per share, of 14.8. A comparison with price-earnings ratios of modern companies may not be straightforward because of the absence of corporation tax and because of the low levels of income tax by twentieth-century standards. The Grand Junction Railway appears to be typical of high-quality 'blue chip' companies with fully operating railway lines between major population centres. Table 16 shows the yields of some of the leading companies in October 1845.

The yields illustrated in Table 16 suggest that the valuations of leading railway shares were not generally excessive by the standards of the valuations of the dot-coms in the late 1990s; indeed, given the speculative climate of the times, they were surprisingly cautious. One possible explanation is that investors in the major companies believed that once the lines had achieved a certain level of profitability there would be little further growth. The very high valuations of the dot-coms in the 1990s (the S&P 500 Index was trading on a price-earnings ratio of over 35 during 1999) may

---

15   See 'When America sneezes', *The Economist*, 6 January 2001, p. 72.

Table 16 **Dividends and dividend yields of selected railway companies, October 1845**

	Share price	Dividend %	Yield %
London & South Western	81	8.0	9.88
York & North Midland	118	10.0	8.47
South Eastern	44	3.725	8.47
London & Brighton	71	4.2	5.92
Manchester & Leeds	154	8.0	5.19
Great Western	163	8.0	4.91
Liverpool & Manchester	213	10.0	4.69
London & Birmingham	220	10.0	4.55
Grand Junction	241	10.0	4.15
Sheffield & Manchester	146	3.2	2.19

Source: *Economist Railway Monitor.*

have reflected a belief that profits growth was likely to take place at a high rate indefinitely. During the railway mania of 1845 the expectation may have been that once a line had been established its profits were likely only to increase modestly in the future. This would explain why the established lines were valued as if they were 'old economy' stocks while the very high valuations were given to lines that were in the process of completion and whose profits had yet to reach the maximum expected. On the other hand, the bubble railways planned in the 1840s seemed to presuppose a high rate of economic growth continuing indefinitely. But given real GDP growth of 7 per cent in 1846, this may have been an assumption that many investors were prepared to make.

The *Railway Monitor*'s review of the market confirms that there was much excited trading in new railway companies. This can be seen as much from the price quotations as from the market commentary. Of about 194 railway companies whose shares were quoted, only 34 had lines open to traffic, and some of the premiums paid on railways that in the event were never built were phenomenal. For example, the £60 shares of the South Wales Railway, which at the time had no lines authorised or built, and with £2.50 paid, were traded in the London and Liverpool stock exchanges in the week previous to 4 October at between £5 5s 8d and £7 1s 4d – representing premiums of 125 per cent and 190 per cent. There were also a number of highly speculative lines that were intended to provide 'direct' cross-country routes. For example, shares in the Great Eastern & Western Railway, which was planned to link Norfolk and South Wales, were quoted as £3 1s 2d with only £2 1s 2d paid – a premium of 40 per cent.

In the same way that the ICT bubble increased interest in stock market investment, the railway manias led to stock market investment becoming popular with people who had never invested in shares before. For example, the economic historian M. C. Reed has shown that women were an important class of railway investor. In 1845, women owned 16 per cent by value of the shareholdings in the Liverpool & Manchester Railway.[16]

EBR and ICT bubble companies

The *Railway Monitor* also reported details of attempts to promote some ventures that with hindsight can be seen to have had little chance of being realised, at least within the then foreseeable future. For example, it described with enthusiasm attempts to form a railway equivalent of the M25 which would circle London.[17] But the so-called Metropolitan Junction Railway was not the only, or the

---

16   Reed, 1975, op. cit., Table 13, p. 123. The following year the Liverpool & Manchester Railway was to become part of the L&NWR.

17   *Economist Railway Monitor*, 4 October 1845, p. 957.

Table 17 **Railway bubble companies of the 1840s**

Company	Rationale	Result
Southern Counties Union	Bristol and Bath to Dover direct	Never built
Grand London and Dublin Approximation Railway	London to Bangor and Holyhead via Stratford on Avon, Worcester, and Shrewsbury	Never built
Irish West Coast Railway	Limerick to Sligo	Never built
Leeds & Edinburgh Direct Atmospheric	Leeds to Edinburgh direct	Atmospheric – defunct high technology
Metropolitan Junction Railway	Round London 'M25' railway	Never built
South London Suburban Railway	Atmospheric railway – Kensington to Dulwich via Clapham and Morden	Atmospheric – defunct high technology
Great Eastern and Western Railway	Yarmouth to Swansea direct line	Never built
Cambridge and Oxford Railway	Cambridge and Oxford direct line	Never built
British and Irish Union Railway	Dumfries to Port Patrick and Stranraer	
The London Railway	Overhead 'atmospheric' railway between London terminuses – equivalent of the Circle Line.	Atmospheric – defunct high technology
Bristol & Liverpool Junction	Direct route between Bristol and Liverpool including bridge over the Severn at Aust then joining existing track at Hereford.	Tunnel under the Severn opened in 1886
Grand Union	Nottingham to the Wash	Never built
Royal Grand Junction	Reigate to Slough	Never built
London, Salisbury & Yeovil	'Central' route to the West of England	Built as part of the London & South Western Railway – opened in 1859
Great Welsh Junction Railway	Bangor to Swansea via Shrewsbury	Never built

Sources: *Economist Railway Monitor*, *Railway Times*.

most flamboyant, of the bubble companies that were launched in the mid-1840s only to rapidly disappear. Table 17 lists a selection of companies whose promoters sought the support of optimistic investors with details of what they planned and their eventual fate.

It is worth analysing why the companies failed when others succeeded, and whether there are any lessons for the dot-com bubble. Perhaps the most obvious point is that none of these railways was obviously impracticable. Indeed, by the end of the nineteenth century, when the railway system was at its most dense with 20,000 miles of line, a significant proportion of these 'bubble' railways must have been replicated in some form or another.

Take, for example, the London Railway, apparently one of the wilder fantasies of the bubble promoters. It was planned to be an 'atmospheric' overhead railway connecting the London mainline termini. Atmospheric railways were a defective railway technology which involved a series of pumping stations that evacuated a pipe laid between the lines to which a piston was attached that drew a train behind it. Unfortunately, the technology was unworkable because it proved impossible to maintain the vacuum in the tube, and the last atmospheric railway in England was converted to standard locomotive traction in the late 1840s when it became clear that the technical problems could not be solved.[18]

The London Railway was proposed with capital of £5 million (£250 million in approximate 2003 values, or equivalent to

18   See C. Hadfield, *Atmospheric Railways*, David & Charles, Newton Abbot, 1967. In addition, there were difficulties in moving trains across points and between stretches of track governed by different pumping stations. In principle, the theory was sound, as conventional locomotive traction requires the engine to pull itself in addition to the payload. Atmospheric railways anticipated electric trains, which also separate power generation from traction. A Paris to Versailles atmospheric railway survived until 1860.

£14 billion as a proportion of 2002 UK GDP) in October 1845, just before the bursting of the bubble, and was never pursued. John Francis, the Victorian railway historian, cited the example of 'railway streets in London with carriages overhead and foot passengers and shopkeepers underneath'[19] as an example of an extreme form of bubble enterprise. But by 1884 the Inner Circle Line was performing the function planned for the London Railway, and in due course was converted to electric traction, which shared the principle of separating power generation from traction with atmospheric railways. The idea of overhead railways also became well established as an alternative to underground railways. Cities such as New York and Chicago have substantial overhead railways, although London does not.

But the important conclusion to be drawn from these examples of bubble railways is not that they were the crazy imaginings of rogues and fantasists, but rather that many were literally 'in advance of their time'. One important factor which appears to have misled many entrepreneurs and investors was that the rate of economic growth immediately before and during the bubble period was very high. Had economic growth been maintained at the high rate of the early 1840s, then many of the bubble railways might not have been so crazy. As it is, the ridicule heaped on the bubble companies by the early railway historian John Francis in 1851 seems misplaced, as equivalents of even the apparently more bizarre schemes were built only decades later. An over-optimistic view of future economic growth may also have been a factor in leading railway companies to misjudge the potential profitability of branch lines and extension railways.

---

19   Francis, op. cit., vol. II, p. 143.

Many of the collapsed dot-com companies share characteristics with the defunct railway companies described above, beyond their similar fate. Take, for example, two companies whose failure has been documented, boo.com and ValueAmerica.[20] Both companies had business plans that were not obviously flawed. Boo.com, founded by Ernst Malmsten and the model Kajsa Leander, was based on the assumption that many people would want to buy sports and fashion clothes on the Internet. At the time the company was launched it was unclear whether this assumption was correct. Boo.com's failure demonstrated that the hopes of the founders and investors were exaggerated. But this did not mean that it was irrational for investors to attempt to discover the degree to which fashion and sports clothes could be sold over the Internet.

Similar considerations apply to ValueAmerica, which was founded by an American businessman, Craig Winn, as an online retail department store which would allow customers to buy almost all household goods. The difference between ValueAmerica and other online retailers was that it would cover a large range of goods which would be delivered directly to customers from the manufacturers without the need for warehouses. As with boo.com, the business proved unworkable and the company collapsed. But again, it was not clear that the business plan was unsound when the company was launched.

One lesson of the railway mania of the 1840s is that the reason for the failure of many bubble railway companies was that they lacked the complementary skills and resources needed

---

20   E. Malmsten, E. Portanger and C. Drazin, *boo hoo*, Random House, 2001; J. D. Kuo, *dot.bomb*, Little, Brown, 2001.

for their success. A bridge over or tunnel under the Severn was perhaps only practicable given the increased traffic as a result of an additional twenty or thirty years' economic growth. Only an economy much larger than that of Britain in the 1840s could have sustained the Metropolitan Junction Railway. Similarly, an inner London circle line became a workable and practicable project in the 1880s or 1890s, but certainly this was not the case in the 1840s. It is almost as if an entrepreneur has to face two questions: *which* projects are practicable and *when* will they be practicable? It was perhaps easy to establish that at some stage an inner London circle line would be a workable project; it was much more difficult to accurately discern when.

The necessary complementary skills and resources can be varied. In some cases, the necessary capital may not be available because of more attractive alternative projects. In other cases, the necessary skills and technologies may not be available. Or, in the case of atmospheric railways, what appeared to be an exciting new technology was later revealed to be defective. But the presence or absence of the necessary complementary factors can only be discovered by a trial-and-error process. The failure of ValueAmerica to establish itself may have reflected the inability of manufacturers to learn the necessary skills for dealing with an online 'warehouseless' department store. It may also have reflected the failure of consumers to discover in sufficient numbers the convenience of being able to shop online for a multiplicity of different goods.

John Cassidy, in his book *dot.con*,[21] suggests that the Internet revolution was merely a passing fad based on the false assumption that it was a revolutionary new business model.[22] But this

---

21   J. Cassidy, *dot.con*, Allen Lane, 2002.
22   Ibid., p. 316.

judgement appears certainly premature and probably too harsh. While it may be correct, the trial-and-error discovery procedure of the market has probably not had enough time to deliver a definitive judgement – if such a definitive once-and-for-all judgement is ever possible. It may take a long time before a 'killer ap'[23] is invented, and before businesses and consumers become adept at using it.

Creating 'irrational exuberance' 1845 and 1999

Is there evidence that the precipitating causes of the EBR bubble of the 1840s and the ICT bubble of the late 1990s were similar? There appear to be three factors that the two periods have in common: economic growth was rapid; real and nominal interest rates were low; and a new technology promised to have significant long-run effects on the economy. Figure 17 compares real economic growth in the UK between 1838 and 1850 and in the USA between 1992 and 2001. The bars represent annual rates of growth and are over-laid so that the ends of rapid economic growth in each cycle, respectively 1846 and 2000, share the same position on the graph. In both cases economic growth was rapid, peaking in the UK at 7 per cent in 1846 and in the US at 4.3 per cent in 1994. Over the relevant periods, growth in the UK was more volatile than in the United States. Also, over the ten years 1838–47 growth in the UK averaged 2.1 per cent whilst over the decade 1992–2001 US growth averaged 3.4 per cent. Nonetheless, the 'large' railway mania of the 1840s and the ICT boom in the US in the 1990s were accompanied by rapid rates of economic growth which may have encouraged

---

23   A 'killer ap' is a very successful application software program.

Figure 17 **Economic growth: UK 1840s and US 1990s**

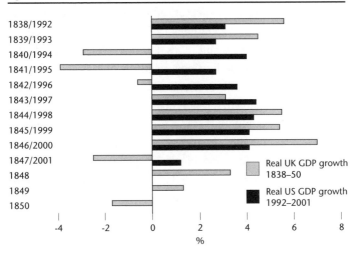

Sources: US 1992–2001: NIPA GDP ($bn Chained $, SAAR) BEA Table 1.10, line 1 (1996 prices); UK 1838–50: B. R. Mitchell, *British Historical Statistics*, Cambridge University Press, 1988, 'National Accounts', Table 6.

investors to believe that prosperity could be maintained for a long period in the 'new era'.

In Britain the boom of the 1840s was marked by a remarkable easing of 'social tension'. The economic historian W. W. Rostow, in his book *British Economy of the Nineteenth Century*,[24] calculated a 'Social Tension Index' which was designed to explain social unrest. The index combines an assessment of business activity with one for the price of wheat. Thus on a scale of 0 to 5 a high level of business activity would be given a value of 5 and a year of depression zero. Similarly a year of high wheat prices would be given a value of zero

24 W. W. Rostow, *British Economy of the Nineteenth Century*, Oxford, 1948, pp. 123ff.

and a year of low wheat prices five. While Rostow's Social Tension Index was intended to predict (or rather, retro-dict) social unrest, it turns out to be remarkably effective in predicting the stock market bubbles of the 1830s and 1840s. For example, the Index had a value of two in 1840, indicating a relatively high degree of social tension, but rose steadily to ten in 1845, the year of the peak of the bubble, before falling to seven in 1846 and two in 1847.

The railway bubble of 1845 was preceded by a period of sharply falling real and nominal interest rates. The nominal yield on 3 per cent Consols, the 'three percents', dropped from 3.4 per cent in 1840 to 3 per cent in 1845. The fall in the real yield was even more dramatic. Because of falling prices in the four years 1840–43, the real yield on Consols reached 11.6 per cent in 1842, but then dropped to 8.6 per cent in 1843, 0.1 per cent in 1844 and 1.3 per cent in 1845. This fall in real and nominal yields made investments in railway securities extremely attractive as they had high actual and prospective yields.

The low interest rates of the mid-1840s had the effect of reducing annuity rates and led to the Brontë sisters investing in railway shares. According to a letter of Charlotte Brontë's in April 1845, the sisters had considered buying annuities, although as they were all under 30 they rejected the idea as the rates were too low – 4.5 per cent at age 25 and 5 per cent at 30. They did, however, invest in the shares of the York & North Midland Railway, which paid a dividend of 10 per cent in 1845, producing a yield of about 9.8 per cent in April 1845 without any loss of principal. With 3 per cent Consols near par and yielding 3 per cent, it is understandable that the Brontë sisters, and many like them, should prefer railway shares.[25]

25 T. J. Wise and J. A. S. Brotherton (eds), *The Brontës, Their Lives, Friendships and Correspondence in Four Volumes*, vol. II, Basil Blackwell, 1932, pp. 31–2. The

The ICT stock market boom of the 1990s was not accompanied in the USA by the sort of dramatic cuts in interest rates that appear to have stimulated the railway mania of the 1840s in Britain. Although short-term and long-term interest rates fell as the boom developed, the rate cuts were not on the same scale as those in the period 1842–5 in Britain. Fed Funds were 6 per cent in 1995, falling to 4.75 per cent in 1999, but long-term rates showed no clearly discernible trend, falling from 6.6 per cent in 1995 to 6.3 per cent in 1999. Although long-term bond yields had been as high as 8.6 per cent in 1990, they had fallen to 6.6 per cent in 1993. But two factors underpinned the ICT boom in addition to the rapid economic growth identified above. First, the inflation rate was low and stable; it averaged 3 per cent in the eleven years 1990–2000 and only 2.3 per cent in the period 1995–9. The second factor was the perceived existence of the so-called 'Greenspan put'. This was the suspicion, almost certainly incorrect, that the Federal Reserve would cut interest rates whenever the stock market fell – thus putting a floor under stock market values. But belief in the 'Greenspan put' gave equity investors a degree of confidence which they would not have had otherwise and contributed to the boom in equity prices.

In contrast to Britain in the 1840s, where interest rates fell sharply, investors in America in the 1990s were convinced that interest rates were unlikely to increase significantly because of the Federal Reserve's success in containing inflation, and they

Brontës' investment in Hudson's York & North Midland Railway proved to be a complete disaster. From a price of around £119 in June 1845, the £50 par shares fell to a low point of £14.90 in April 1850, a discount of 70 per cent to their par value. By 1852, the shares had recovered to £25, and in 1854 the company was part of a major amalgamation as part of the North Eastern Railway group and the shares traded at the equivalent of £27.50. The £50 shares were consolidated into £100 shares in May/June 1852 and their actual 'exit' price was £55.

believed that, should the stock market fall, the Fed would intervene to prevent a serious market collapse. Thus both periods share both high rates of economic growth and favourable interest rate regimes, albeit different in character.

Bubble trouble

Does the EBR bubble of 1845–6 have any implications for the debate on whether central banks should attempt to prevent the creation of bubbles?[26] The EBR bubble of the 1840s has particular relevance for bubbles associated with new technologies like ICT. According to the Austrian analysis, described in Chapter 4, monetary mismanagement has the effect of concentrating entrepreneurial experiments into a short period. A prevailing interest rate lower than the natural rate will also inject false information into the system, leading entrepreneurs to make unnecessary experiments on the basis of there being more capital available than is actually the case. It follows that bubbles like those of the 1840s and 1990s may generate so much unrealistic optimism that resources are wasted in the trial-and-error process. While this is undoubtedly the case, it is easy to exaggerate the amount of waste. The effect of a bubble may be to concentrate the process of experiment, which otherwise would have taken place over a much longer period of time, into a very short period. In addition, some of the information gained that may not have immediate relevance may become valuable, as we have seen, at a much later stage. While the concept of the overhead railway may have been totally impractic-

---

26   See also M. Friedman and C. A. E. Goodhart, *Money, Inflation and the Constitutional Position of the Central Bank,* Institute of Economic Affairs, London, 2003.

able in the 1840s, the development of the concept meant that it was available when it did become practicable with the invention of electric traction later in the nineteenth century.

It follows that to a very large degree the trial-and-error process results in genuinely useful new information about the commercial application of the new technology. To a significant degree bubbles are not wasteful processes. Only on the assumption of perfect knowledge can the process generally be said to waste resources. The destruction of resources more often than not is the price to be paid for discovering how the new technology can and cannot be applied commercially.

The fact that the bubble is part of the trial-and-error discovery process suggests that central banks should not be too concerned about the creation of bubbles that involve new technology. As the previous section shows, technology bubbles appear to require a number of factors – a new technology, a lengthy period of rapid economic growth, price stability and either sharply falling interest rates or an understanding that the stock market will be supported by interest rate cuts if it shows signs of weakness. Of these factors, only interest rate policy is in the hands of the central bank. The Bank of England in the 1840s can be criticised for the sharp falls in interest rates that coincided with the inflation of the bubbles. Similarly, the Federal Reserve can be blamed for allowing belief in the 'Greenspan put' to become established. However, it is probably a mistake to think that the central bank can prevent the creation of 'irrational exuberance'. For example, the long periods of high economic growth in the 1840s and the 1990s were a major factor in causing belief in the 'new era' and consequently an important factor in creating the bubble. Further, no central bank could have reasonably intervened to thwart the falling wheat prices of the

1840s or the price stability of the 1990s in order to prevent a bubble developing. It follows that sometimes bubbles are the price of developing new technologies.

What happened after the railway manias?

How would an investor have fared if he had invested in railway shares at various stages between 1827 and 1850? Figure 18 shows an index of railway shares between May 1827 and December 1868, together with the 'Hayek' Industrial Share Index of share prices generally over the same period. It also shows the same 'Hayek' index rebased on the railway share index in January 1841 and January 1850. These latter two dates represent respectively a time before the 'large' railway mania began and the nadir of railway share prices after the bubble burst. The figure shows that a railway investor would have outperformed the 'Hayek' index had he invested when investment in railways became possible in 1827. However, had he invested in 1841, before the onset of the 'large' railway mania, and in 1851, when railway shares reached their low point after the bursting of the bubble, his investment would have been less satisfactory than an investment in shares generally, represented by the 'Hayek' Industrial Share Index.

Of course, the index shows average values, and individual shares showed significant variations round the mean. For example, the London Brighton and South Coast Railway (LB&SCR) started the 1850s at around £80, subsequently rising to around £120, but by the end of the 1860s it had sunk to around £50. Although the LB&SCR had a well-defined territory connecting Brighton and the south coast to London, with considerable commuter traffic, the company was squeezed to the west by the L&SWR and to the east

Figure 18 **Railway and all sector share indices, 1827–68**

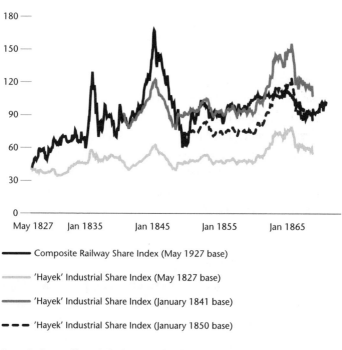

Source: See Annex to Chapter 5. The Composite Railway Share index is composed of the GRS and Miller Railway Share Indices.

by the South Eastern Railway. Its directors sought to expand the company, doubling its capital to £16 million, but the result was an erosion of profitability and the company nearly collapsed in 1867. Another company that only surmounted its problems with difficulty was the GWR. As we have seen, the company adopted an aggressive strategy, attempting to establish a broad-gauge territory as far as the Mersey in competition with the L&NWR. The result was a highly geared company whose shares languished through-out the whole eighteen-year period from 1850 to 1868. The shares were £69 in January 1850 and only £48.75 in December 1868. In 1869, the company was nearly bankrupt and made an unsuccess-ful appeal to the government for assistance. Twice over the period, the shares sank to just over £40 before recovering.

But some companies performed better than the average. These include the Midland Railway, whose shares were at £44.75 in Janu-ary 1850 but had climbed to £112.50 by December 1868. Another strong performer was the Lancashire and Yorkshire, whose shares advanced from £58 (adjusted for calls) to £127.90. Other leading companies, such as the L&NWR and the L&SWR, showed little net change over the period.

Annex: share price indices

The indices used for nineteenth-century share prices quoted in this chapter are with two exceptions derived from A. D. Gayer, W. W. Rostow and A. J. Schwartz, *The Growth and Fluctuation of the British Economy 1790–1850*, vol. I, Oxford, 1953, pp. 368ff. The authors constructed monthly capitalisation weighted share price indices for the following series:

Gayer, Rostow & Schwartz (GRS) Indices

	——— *Period* ———	
	Start	*End*
Share prices (i.e. all sector index)	January 1811	December 1850
Share prices excluding mines	January 1811	December 1850
Canal shares	January 1811	December 1850

Dock shares	January 1811	December 1850
Waterworks shares	January 1811	December 1850
Insurance shares	January 1811	December 1850
Gaslight & coke shares	January 1819	December 1850
Railway shares	May 1827	December 1850
Joint stock banks	January 1831	December 1850

GRS Railway Share Index

In the case of the railway share index, the constituent companies are as follows:

	——— Period ———	
	Start	*End*
Liverpool and Manchester	May 1827	March 1836
Stockton & Darlington	January 1828	December 1834
Cheltenham	May 1827	March 1836
Forest of Dean	May 1827	February 1832
London & Birmingham	June 1833	August 1846
Great Western	September 1835	December 1850
London & Greenwich	January 1835	December 1850
Bristol & Exeter	March 1836	December 1850
Manchester and Leeds	November 1836	July 1847
North Eastern	January 1838	July 1847
London and Southwestern	November 1839	December 1850
Midland Counties	January 1841	December 1850
Edinburgh & Glasgow	January 1842	December 1850
Great North of England	January 1841	December 1850

(Gayer et al., op. cit., vol. I, p. 361. Reprinted by permission of the Oxford University Press.)

Miller Railway Share Index

There being no index of railway shares after December 1850, the author constructed a monthly index of railway shares from January 1850 until December 1870. Share prices of five large railway companies were used to construct a monthly simple-average index, unweighted by capitalisation. Share prices were taken from the end-month edition of *The Economist*. The index is less than ideal, because it is not capitalisation weighted and includes only railway companies that had a continuous existence over the whole period. Nonetheless, it gives a general impression of the movement in the prices of railway shares. The five constituent companies are as follows: the London and Southwestern Railway, the Great Western Railway, the London & North Western Railway, the London Brighton & South Coast Railway, and the Midland Railway. The index thus represents 'blue chips' and not the shares of the smaller companies.

Hayek Industrial Share Index

The Hayek index is an unweighted monthly index of industrial share prices covering the period January 1820 to December 1868, and hence overlaps with the GRS All Sector Index. The index was constructed by Professor F. A. Hayek, following a commission by General Dawes, to show how industrial shares behaved in the trade cycle. As a result it excludes banks, insurance and bridge companies. The sub-groups making up the index include canals, docks, waterworks, gaslight and coke companies, British mines, railways and miscellaneous companies. Further details and index numbers are to be found in Gayer et al., op. cit., vol. I, pp. 455ff.

The Miller Railway Share and Hayek indices differ from such

modern indices as the FTSE 100 and the NASDAQ in that they are not capitalisation weighted and consequently are at risk of giving too much weight to small and medium-sized companies. However, in the case of the Miller Railway Share Index, this risk is reduced by the index including five of the largest railway companies.

One major difficulty with the GRS Railway Share Index, which covers the period of the two bubbles, is that, because it is focused on the shares of large companies, it may not capture all the 'exuberance' of the two railway share bubbles. The GRS Railway Share Index stands in contrast to the NASDAQ and FTSE Tech-MARK indices, which include very large numbers of small ICT companies whose share prices may have reflected greater exuberance than did the established companies. Thus a modern equivalent of the GRS Railway Share Index would include only large ICT companies such as Microsoft, Cisco Systems, Dell, Vodafone and IBM. It would not have included such bubble companies as E-Toys, ValueAmerica or boo.com.

6 REGULATING THE NEXT BIG THING

Path dependence

The fact that the ICT revolution involves increasing returns to scale and 'path dependence' has led some economists to argue that the 'New Economy' is subject to pervasive market failure and requires intervention to correct it. In particular, the economists Brian Arthur and Paul Krugman have argued that because ICT has caused an economic revolution it means that the 'New Economy' is subject to economic laws different from those that rule the 'Old Economy'.[1] As a result there is a new kind of market failure which needs correction by government or judicial action.

Professor Arthur divides modern economies into two parts. First, there is the 'Old Economy', the 'Halls of Production', which is governed by decreasing returns and is subject to conventional economic analysis. In the 'Old Economy', any increase in production rapidly runs into increasing costs and declining revenues. Here business success will tend to be achieved by economising on costs, and competition will force prices towards the average cost of production. Arthur gives the example of coffee production:

> ... if a coffee plantation expanded production it would

---

1   W. B. Arthur, 'Increasing Returns and the New World of Business', *Harvard Business Review*, July/August 1996; P. Krugman, *Peddling Prosperity: Economic Sense and Nonsense in the Age of Diminished Expectations*, Norton, 1994.

ultimately be driven to use land less suitable for coffee – it would run into diminishing returns. So if coffee plantations competed, each would expand until it ran into limitations in the form of rising costs or diminishing profits. The market would be shared by many plantations, and a market would be established at a predictable level – depending on tastes for coffee and the availability of suitable farmland. Planters would produce coffee so long as doing so was profitable, but because the price would be squeezed down to the average cost of production, no one would make a killing.[2]

The 'Old Economy', he argues, is marked by management in hierarchies and complex administration, which optimise existing lines of production. Improvements are incremental and there is no search for the revolutionary 'next big thing'. The 'Old Economy' is that of the traditional economics of the textbooks – the world of Alfred Marshall.

In contrast, Arthur argues, the 'New Economy' is marked by 'increasing returns' and 'positive feedback'. In the new technology industries, the more widely a new technology is adopted the more valuable it becomes, and potentially the more profitable to the provider. Thus a fax machine is of no value if there is only one in existence, but as more and more people own them they become more useful and valuable. These increasing returns are particularly, but not exclusively, prevalent in networks both actual and virtual. In other words, increasing returns apply to physical networks such as the Internet or virtual networks such as computer operating systems or video standards like Betamax or VHS. So far the analysis is uncontroversial, but then Arthur claims that, because of some accident of history, an inferior standard can be 'locked in', and

2   Arthur, op. cit., p. 2.

consumers have no choice but to use a less than optimal product if a dominant company has succeeded in cornering the market.

Arthur gives a number of examples where inferior technologies have been foisted on consumers as a result of historical accident or by companies using established positions to 'leverage' success in one technology into dominance in another. One of the examples most used by the proponents of such inferior technology 'lock-ins' is the QWERTY keyboard, which has survived the transition from typewriter to personal computer. Paul Krugman uses the title 'Qwerty World' for one of the chapters in his book *Peddling Prosperity*, and suggests that such inefficiencies are common in the 'New Economy'.[3] These ideas have been very influential, and Brian Arthur's work is known to have been a major influence on the former US Assistant Attorney General, Joel Klein, and the Department of Justice's anti-trust suit against Microsoft. Microsoft, it is alleged, has used its dominance in the operating system market to 'leverage' a similar dominant position for its Internet Explorer Web browser by including it on the Windows desktop. As a result, Microsoft obtained an unfair head start over its rivals. Arthur compares the position to the land rushes in Oklahoma or Kansas in the 1880s, and claims that the position of a dominant company such as Microsoft would be the same as if everyone starts off with horses and buggies but then,

> … if you had won three or four of these races in succession
> and you parlayed your winnings into buying a Toyota Land
> cruiser instead of a horse and buggy. And just to make
> doubly sure, you hobble everybody else's horse at night.[4]

---

3   Krugman, op. cit.
4   W. B. Arthur and D. Gates, 'The PreText Interview', *PreText Magazine*, May 1998, p. 6. Available on [http:///www.pretext.com/may98/columns/interview.htm].

The resulting market dominance, Arthur claims, is both unfair and liable to lead to a 'lock-in' of an inferior technology as the owner of the locked-in franchise has no strong incentive to continue to innovate. Thus Microsoft took ten years to '… come out with a decent version of Windows'.[5]

However, Arthur and the other exponents of 'path dependence' and 'lock-in' have been criticised on the grounds that the historical examples of inferior technology 'lock-in' used turn out to be myths. For example, it appears that QWERTY keyboards are not inferior. Professors Stan Leibowitz and Stephen Margolis have discovered that in the 1880s and 1890s, when the typewriter business was first developing, there were numerous competitive keyboards and the QWERTY board was at least as satisfactory as any of its competitors. Similarly, tests of the vaunted Dvorak keyboard showed that it had no obvious superiority over the QWERTY board.[6] What is particularly significant is that there were numerous typewriter technologies in competition in the 1880s and 1890s, and there is no reason to believe that the market selected the wrong one.

Leibowitz and Margolis explain why lock-in is unlikely. They use a table constructed by Brian Arthur to show how lock-in can come about to illustrate the strategies used by consumers to avoid being forced to adopt inferior technology. Table 18 below, reproduced from an article by Brian Arthur, appears to show how it is all too easy for consumers to adopt inferior technology.

It appears from the pay-offs shown in Table 18 that consumers

---

5   Ibid., p. 7.
6   S. Leibowitz and S. Margolis, 'Policy and Path Dependence from QWERTY to Windows 95', *Regulation*, vol. 18, no. 3, 1995, pp. 3ff. Available on [http://www.cato.org/pubs/regulation/reg18n3d.html].

Table 18 **Adoption pay-offs**

Number of previous adoptions	0	10	20	30	40	50	60	70	80	90
Technology A	10	11	12	13	14	15	16	17	18	19
Technology B	4	7	10	13	16	19	22	25	28	31

are led inevitably to choose Technology A because of the high initial pay-offs resulting from its adoption. But this is inefficient if the number of adopters is large; if there are 100 adopters, the pay-off for Technology B is greater than for Technology A. But Leibowitz and Margolis point out that this analysis is oversimplified. If, for example, Technology B were protected by patents or copyrights, and if the number of potential adopters were large, then the owner of Technology B would have a motive to cut the initial price (or offer other incentives) to establish it as the technology of choice. In this way, the initial disadvantages of adopting Technology B, as illustrated in Table 18, could be overcome. Leibowitz and Margolis explain that there are means by which consumers can adopt the superior technology although faced with the pay-offs illustrated. If the technology is not patentable, the owners can develop variants which are. The owners can advertise, they can lease the new technology, or they can enter into strategic alliances.

But most important, given the table of pay-offs illustrated, it does not follow that consumers will inevitably choose the inferior Technology A. Consumers are not passive when confronted with a choice between new technologies. They are quite capable of responding to the whole table of pay-offs rather than just the first few, as Arthur's argument seems to suggest they will. Consumers are not inert and without foresight, but can anticipate future developments and pay-offs. In the case of Microsoft and Apple, this appears to be exactly what happened.

In the early 1980s Apple computers may have had significant technical advantages over the first IBM PCs with Microsoft DOS operating systems. But consumers may have seen that the Microsoft system was capable of development into the different versions of Windows that have appeared since. However, those who bought IBM PCs in the early 1980s may have had factors other than technical performance in mind. Purchasers for businesses in particular may have considered that reliability and continuity in servicing were important. They preferred to use software supplied by a company that had a strategic alliance with IBM rather than Apple, which was (relatively) small and, given the rapidly changing market, might easily go out of business. As was said at the time: 'Nobody gets sacked for buying IBM.'

One puzzle for Brian Arthur is to explain how formerly dominant software such as Lotus 123 and Wordperfect were replaced by Microsoft equivalents. These apparent counter-examples to the theory of 'lock-in' are explained away as the 'next big thing'. So great are the advantages, it is implied, of Excel and Word that they could easily displace previously dominant software. But in reality there is very little difference between the displacement of word processing and spreadsheet software and operating systems. Different software is different software and not the 'next big thing'.

The standard gauge 'lock-in' and Microsoft

What lessons can be learnt from the apparent lock-in of the standard gauge in the last century? The competition offered to the standard gauge by the GWR's broad gauge and the replacement of the latter in 1892 anticipates in slow motion some of the main features of the software standard 'wars' of the 1980s, 1990s and 2000s.

As we have seen, the decision to adopt the 4 ft 8½ in gauge for the S&DR was not based on any calculation of the most efficient gauge for a railway; rather Stephenson adopted the gauge for horse-drawn railways used in collieries in the North-east of England. This gauge was apparently based on the breadth of farm carts pulled by two horses abreast. The standard gauge was then adopted by most other railways in the British Isles, with the exception of those in Ireland and those parts of the west of England and Wales dominated by the GWR and its satellite companies.

In the case of the GWR, as we have seen, Brunel consciously decided to adopt the 7 ft ¼ in gauge on the grounds that it was technically superior to the standard gauge as it was suitable for trains with a lower centre of gravity and larger wheels which, he argued, would reduce friction. Although he believed that a gauge broader than 4 ft 8½ ins was desirable, he appears to have made no attempt to calculate the ideal broad gauge and rather to have used the 7ft ¼ in gauge that his father, Sir Marc Brunel, had used for a horse-drawn railway in a sawmill that he managed in Battersea. Indeed, when asked whether he had any regrets about the use of the broad gauge, he replied that if anything he would have preferred to have adopted an even broader gauge.

But is the adoption of the standard gauge an example of the lock-in of an inferior technology as described by Brian Arthur and other supporters of path-dependency theories? While the broad gauge may have had some advantages, these were offset by its extra expense – wider tunnels, cuttings, bridges and embankments, and the extra land required. The tests carried out by the Gauge Commission in November 1845 showed clearly that broad-gauge trains could pull heavier loads faster than their standard-gauge rivals.[7] However, it seems that this superiority was the result of the technical superiority of the GWR engines rather than that of the broad gauge. It is unclear to what degree the broad gauge was technically superior to the standard gauge, and it is still disputed by experts. For example, the railway historian Tim Bryan concludes in a recent study of the broad gauge that experts are still as divided on its merits as they were in the 1850s.[8]

However, even if it is granted that the broad gauge had significant technical advantages over the standard gauge, it does not follow that the eventual adoption of the standard gauge represented an example of market failure. The standard gauge was adopted by the Liverpool & Manchester Railway, which received its authorising Act in 1826, and subsequently by the Grand Junction Railway and the L&BR, which were authorised in 1833. It was only in 1835 that the GWR was authorised (after a failed attempt in 1834), and the GWR board accepted Brunel's plan to build the railway on the broad gauge. The fact that the standard gauge was adopted by the main national trunk route linking London, Birmingham, Liverpool and Manchester is consequently not a sign of market failure. That the Stephensons, father and son, did not consider using a broader gauge may be a sign of the weakness of their engineering imagination, but not of market failure.

But there is another reason why the standard gauge came to dominate the national system, even if one grants the broad gauge considerable technical superiority over the standard gauge. Unlike

---

7   MacDermot, op. cit., vol. I, part I, p. 231.

8   Bryan, op. cit., p. 52. An example of a vigorous opponent of the broad gauge is A. Vaughan, Brunel's biographer. See his *Isambard Kingdom Brunel, Engineering Knight-Errant*, John Murray, 1991.

computer software, where the costs of conversion from one system to another are symmetrical, in the case of railway gauges in England they were different. Thus, it costs the same for computer users to switch from Wordperfect to Word as it does for them to switch from Word to Wordperfect; the software is similarly priced and the skills needed to make the change are much the same. This was not the case once the two railway systems based on the broad and standard gauges had been established. Although it proved expensive for the GWR to convert to the standard gauge (some estimates put the cost of conversion at £3 million – £150 million at approximate 2002 values), a change from the standard to the broad gauge would have been much more expensive in terms of both cash and inconvenience. A change from the standard to the broad gauge would have required at the very least the reconstruction of all tunnels to take the broader-gauge rails and trains. On the other hand, the conversion of broad-gauge lines to narrow did not require any major works except for the relaying of the track.

It follows that the standard gauge had a *technological* lock-in which would have prevented a conversion to the broad gauge unless the technical advantages of the latter were overwhelming. It is interesting that this asymmetric cost of conversion appears to be unique to transport networks, which involve massive sunk costs. It is worth turning the argument on its head. Suppose the broad gauge had been the first on the scene and only a small proportion of the system had succumbed to the standard gauge. Then a change from a clearly technically inferior broad gauge to the standard gauge would have been possible given the relatively low cost of conversion from broad to standard.

The South Wales Railway and the Microsoft anti-trust suit

It is interesting that the early British railway system had developed a mechanism for making such changes where the change was worthwhile. One common assumption of the supporters of the 'lock-in' theory is that consumers and competitors, faced by a dominant standard, react only passively. But this is not necessarily the case. Take the example of the Railway Clearing House (RCH). We have seen (p. 74) how the RCH was established in 1842 by Carr Glyn, chairman of the L&BR, primarily as a means of increasing through-traffic and capturing the resulting network externalities. But the RCH had another important function. This was the introduction of uniform standards for signals and rolling stock. When the railways were first built many adopted different signalling systems, which made movement of traffic across the system inconvenient, if not hazardous. The RCH, on which all member companies were represented, organised a gradual move to compatible signalling systems and wagon couplings. Although the RCH never became involved in the controversy over the broad gauge, the GWR did not become a member until the 1860s; still it had a role in establishing uniform standards of train operating. It is in fact difficult to see how the RCH could have acted to resolve the gauge war, as the GWR could not have been forced into membership or necessarily bound by majority decisions.

Nonetheless, the RCH is a model of how users can collaborate to develop uniform standards and to replace them with superior versions, should that prove necessary. But there is another example of collective action by railway users which demonstrates convincingly how railway users combined to replace an unsatisfactory standard. The South Wales Railway (SWR) had been developed as part of the GWR system, using the broad gauge, and ran from Gloucester to Milford Haven along the south coast of Wales by way of Chepstow and Newport. A major difficulty was that the lines from the Monmouth and Glamorgan coal fields had been built on the standard gauge, so that freight had to be transhipped for onward journeys on the SWR, adding significantly to the cost. In 1866, 269 firms appealed to the SWR board to convert the line to the standard gauge and the request was granted in 1872.

The importance of these examples, and especially the latter, is that they demonstrate how users of a service faced by an uncongenial standard can collaborate to negotiate a better deal with the dominant supplier – or to replace one standard with another.

It is significant that the computer industry has not seen the formation of an organisation with an equivalent standard-setting function to that of the RCH or, more important, any movement amongst a large body of PC users to change collectively to an operating system other than Windows. Despite the existence of the open software movement and the Linux operating system, the fact that there has been no large migration from Microsoft suggests that there is no general dissatisfaction and that computer users are not being forced to use Microsoft products against their will. It is significant that much of the campaigning against Microsoft has been undertaken by its competitors and not by its customers.

Thus the case against Microsoft brought by the US Department of Justice is flawed in terms of the economics, whatever the legal position. The case argued, in essence, that Microsoft imposed its Web browser, Internet Explorer, on an unwilling public by requiring PC manufacturers – so-called Original Equipment Manufacturers (OEMs) – to include it on computer 'desktops'. But there was nothing to prevent computer owners from obtaining Netscape Navigator if they thought it superior to Internet Explorer, and the argument assumes a passivity in the face of an inferior product which appears unwarranted. It is interesting that Netscape Navigator has been almost completely supplanted by Internet Explorer, which is acknowledged to be a superior product.

Government regulation of network standards

Most conventional analyses of the EBR revolution seem to assume that it would have been desirable if the government had imposed a single standard gauge, as it did in Ireland. But it would have been necessary for this to have been done as early as 1835 when the Great Western Railway was seeking parliamentary authority, and at that time it was unclear how great were the disadvantages of a 'break of gauge'. In addition, it could not have been known what the technical advantages, if any, of the broad gauge were over the standard gauge. To argue that the government should have imposed a single standard from the outset is to make a judgement with the benefit of hindsight.

The advantages of having a single standard are obvious, although perhaps easily exaggerated, but the difficulty for any government in imposing a standard is that it has to establish which is the appropriate standard when this may not be clear. An example of the difficulties involved is the decision by the European Commission in the 1990s that the terms of licences for the third generation, 3G, radio spectrum auctioned by member states should require the use of the W-CDMA standard. Unfortunately, as *The Economist* has pointed out, the EU appears to have selected a standard that mobile phone companies are finding very difficult to bring into operation.[9] The intention was to allow users to 'roam' from one country to another, as is possible with GSM, 2G, mobile phones. As a result the introduction of 3G phone networks in Europe may be delayed, which is not the case in other countries where governments have not imposed a standard. Some successful buyers of 3G licences sought to renegotiate their terms and to postpone the launch of 3G services.

But an alternative 3G standard, CDMA2000-1X, was already (late 2002) being used by 17 million people in Japan, South Korea and America. For example, Japan has a fully operating 3G system on the CDMA2000-1X standard which is competing successfully with a W-CDMA system. In addition, China, Australia and a number of countries in South America are considering the CDMA2000-1X standard in preference to W-CDMA.

The difficulty with a government or regulator imposing a network standard is that it is only clear with hindsight which is the correct standard to impose. The danger, illustrated by the EU imposing the W-CDMA standard on 3G phone operators, is that it may select the wrong one.

---

9   'Time for Plan B', *The Economist*, 28 September 2002, pp. 77ff.

7 CONCLUSION: COMPARING THE EBR AND ICT REVOLUTIONS

Conclusions for analysis

The development of the EBRs offers a large number of useful parallels with the ICT revolution. Both were revolutions in communications and involved 'network externalities'. They were carried out under laissez-faire regimes with little government intervention. Furthermore, both revolutions included stock market bubbles, and in the case of the EBRs two boom-and-bust cycles. Other parallels, such as that between the ICT revolution and the US telegraph system, share many of these characteristics but not all.

One major difference between the EBR and ICT revolutions is that the former involved only physical networks while the ICT revolution included both physical and virtual networks. However, the fact that the EBR revolution involved only one type of network means that it is much easier to isolate the factors that influence the private enterprise development of any network. In other words, the EBR revolution can be used as an example to explain some of the otherwise puzzling phenomena of the ICT revolution.

Thus, the advantage of being first in the field is rapidly eroded by competition and participants are forced to defend a 'territory' from interloping competition. Such 'if you're not in, you can't win' and 'winner takes all' strategies further erode profitability. Managers face the dilemma of whether to expand their 'footprint' at the cost of reduced profitability or to surrender territory to a competitor, which may destroy their business. This tension is apparent in both the development of the EBRs and particularly in the telecom companies in their strategy towards the 3G mobile phone auctions.

There are also parallels in the effect on the economy of the EBR and ICT revolutions. Both revolutions involved versions of the 'Solow Productivity Paradox' in their early stages, as it takes some time before the uses of the new technology are discovered and applied. This means that there is a significant lapse of time between the realisation that the new technology has revolutionary possibilities and its full effect on the economy. One important conclusion drawn from the EBR revolution is that the social return tends to greatly exceed the return to investors in the new technology. Only shareholders who are particularly astute will be able to capture a significant share of the social return, which will otherwise go to consumers. The private enterprise development of networks harnesses the enthusiasm of investors to develop a denser network than would be created by a system planned by a central authority, or the directions of a regulator.

In the EBR revolution, shareholders generally did not fare well. Their companies had to contend with competition and the need to dominate a 'territory' and the problem of knowing when the complementary skills and factors would be available to make an investment successful. For example, investors in GWR shares saw them rise to £220 at the height of the bubble in 1845, only to see them fall to just over £40 in 1867. By 1870, the share price recovered to £70, but over the whole period GWR shares were an unsatisfactory investment.

In the right conditions, of low real interest rates and rapid economic growth, both the EBR and ICT revolutions resulted in major stock market bubbles. These reached their respective peaks in 1845 and 2000 and were accompanied by a trial-and-error process that selected the schemes most likely to prove successful businesses. In many cases, with the benefit of hindsight, the proposed businesses can be seen to have been, literally, before their time – lacking the necessary complementary factors and skills. While the booms are in progress, it is unclear which businesses will be successful. There is no guarantee that what appears to be the 'next big thing', atmospheric railways in the 1840s and, perhaps, 3G technology today, will live up to expectations.

Conclusions for policy

It has often been suggested that the EBR revolution was chaotic and wasteful. This conclusion is not supported by the evidence. Unlike in most other countries, in Britain the railway network was built under a laissez-faire regime and very largely without subsidy from the taxpayer. The result was that the British network was denser and constructed more rapidly than that of France, which used central planning to construct its network. In this context, it is also significant that consumers benefited far more from the new railway technology than shareholders.

The railway mania of the 1840s, which has significant similarities to the ICT bubble of the 1990s, suggests that the latter is not a 'dot con' but rather, to a large degree, the trial-and-error method of the market to establish how the new technology can be put to commercial use. A large proportion of the resources used up cannot be said to be wasted as they represent the price paid for discovering how the new technology can be used to satisfy consumers.

Of course, given the exaggerated optimism of the bubble, some possibilities were explored which would not have been attempted in ordinary times. But even in such cases, the knowledge of the commercial practicability of the new technology gained may be valuable. One consequence of bubbles is that they can concentrate an experimental process that otherwise might have taken many years into a short period.

But more important, despite their reputation, the evidence of the EBRs is that a largely unfettered capital market was highly effective in marshalling the resources necessary to equip Britain with an extremely dense railway network in a short space of time without the assistance of the taxpayer. In contrast, France adopted a state system for developing its railway network with the result that the construction of the system was slow and expensive for taxpayers. It is a paradox that the inadequacies of the French railway system were a handicap to the Prussian invaders in 1870. The capital market was also successful in establishing which lines were commercially practicable and which technologies workable. The impression created by such novels as Trollope's *The Way We Live Now* and Dickens's *Little Dorrit*, to the effect that the stock market was both inefficient and largely dishonest, is misplaced. There is no evidence that largely unfettered capital markets have performed any less satisfactorily in the ICT boom, despite the stock market bubble of the late 1990s.

It follows that central banks and governments should not attempt to regulate bubbles out of existence, or even attempt to prevent their occurrence. Bubbles appear to require an exacting set of circumstances to develop, and the resources wasted are probably small in extent although easy to exaggerate.

Another lesson to be drawn from the construction of the British railway network in the mid-nineteenth century is that a largely unregulated framework allowed the successful completion of a series of major projects without subsidy. But more important, the tension between shareholders and promoters meant that there was an inbuilt mechanism to minimise the extravagance and cost overruns that have been so prevalent in twentieth-century state-managed 'mega-projects'. Brunel's extravagance in building the GWR may have been costly to shareholders, but the latter soon learned how to restrain directors from submitting to the blandishments of engineers, landowners and lawyers who had an interest in promoting railways. As we have seen, the relatively sophisticated capital market of the 1840s also proved effective in sorting out which major railway projects could be commercially successful and which not.

The history of the EBRs does not suggest there is any danger of new network technologies subject to increasing returns becoming 'locked in'. Rather it suggests that consumers confronted by an unsatisfactory standard can collaborate for its replacement. It follows that much of the anxiety that Microsoft, for example, might be able to lock in an unsatisfactory operating system, such as Windows, is misplaced. It also follows that the legal action against Microsoft by the US Department of Justice and a number of states has little economic justification.

It also appears that it is a mistake for governments to attempt to set network standards, as it is all too easy for them to establish the wrong one. Freely operating markets can easily find the correct standard through a process of trial and error. Those who maintain that the British government in the nineteenth century should have established a specific gauge as the standard for the national railway network are arguing with the benefit of hindsight. The attempt by the EU to establish W-CDMA as the standard for 3G mobile telephony has proved to be a mistake, and has meant that the introduction of 3G mobile phones has been delayed. Furthermore, the process of competition between standards, while preventing economies of scale initially, leads to the development of better standards than had a uniform standard based on superior technology been adopted from the start.

ABOUT THE IEA

The Institute is a research and educational charity (No. CC 235 351), limited by guarantee. Its mission is to improve understanding of the fundamental institutions of a free society with particular reference to the role of markets in solving economic and social problems.

The IEA achieves its mission by:

- a high-quality publishing programme
- conferences, seminars, lectures and other events
- outreach to school and college students
- brokering media introductions and appearances

The IEA, which was established in 1955 by the late Sir Antony Fisher, is an educational charity, not a political organisation. It is independent of any political party or group and does not carry on activities intended to affect support for any political party or candidate in any election or referendum, or at any other time. It is financed by sales of publications, conference fees and voluntary donations.

In addition to its main series of publications the IEA also publishes a quarterly journal, *Economic Affairs*, and has two specialist programmes – Environment and Technology, and Education.

The IEA is aided in its work by a distinguished international Academic Advisory Council and an eminent panel of Honorary Fellows. Together with other academics, they review prospective IEA publications, their comments being passed on anonymously to authors. All IEA papers are therefore subject to the same rigorous independent refereeing process as used by leading academic journals.

IEA publications enjoy widespread classroom use and course adoptions in schools and universities. They are also sold throughout the world and often translated/reprinted.

Since 1974 the IEA has helped to create a world-wide network of 100 similar institutions in over 70 countries. They are all independent but share the IEA's mission.

Views expressed in the IEA's publications are those of the authors, not those of the Institute (which has no corporate view), its Managing Trustees, Academic Advisory Council members or senior staff.

Members of the Institute's Academic Advisory Council, Honorary Fellows, Trustees and Staff are listed on the following page.

The Institute gratefully acknowledges financial support for its publications programme and other work from a generous benefaction by the late Alec and Beryl Warren.

199

Other papers recently published by the IEA include:

WHO, What and Why?

Transnational Government, Legitimacy and the World Health Organization
Roger Scruton
Occasional Paper 113; ISBN 0 255 36487 3
£8.00

The World Turned Rightside Up

A New Trading Agenda for the Age of Globalisation
John C. Hulsman
Occasional Paper 114; ISBN 0 255 36495 4
£8.00

The Representation of Business in English Literature

Introduced and edited by Arthur Pollard
Readings 53; ISBN 0 255 36491 1
£12.00

Anti-Liberalism 2000

The Rise of New Millennium Collectivism
David Henderson
Occasional Paper 115; ISBN 0 255 36497 0
£7.50

Capitalism, Morality and Markets

Brian Griffiths, Robert A. Sirico, Norman Barry & Frank Field

Readings 54; ISBN 0 255 36496 2

£7.50

A Conversation with Harris and Seldon

Ralph Harris & Arthur Seldon

Occasional Paper 116; ISBN 0 255 36498 9

£7.50

Malaria and the DDT Story

Richard Tren & Roger Bate

Occasional Paper 117; ISBN 0 255 36499 7

£10.00

A Plea to Economists Who Favour Liberty: Assist the Everyman

Daniel B. Klein

Occasional Paper 118; ISBN 0 255 36501 2

£10.00

Waging the War of Ideas

John Blundell

Occasional Paper 119; ISBN 0 255 36500 4

£10.00

The Changing Fortunes of Economic Liberalism
Yesterday, Today and Tomorrow
David Henderson
Occasional Paper 105 (new edition); ISBN 0 255 36520 9
£12.50

The Global Education Industry
Lessons from Private Education in Developing Countries
James Tooley
Hobart Paper 141 (new edition); ISBN 0 255 36503 9
£12.50

Saving Our Streams
*The Role of the Anglers' Conservation Association in
Protecting English and Welsh Rivers*
Roger Bate
Research Monograph 53; ISBN 0 255 36494 6
£10.00

Better Off Out?
The Benefits or Costs of EU Membership
Brian Hindley & Martin Howe
Occasional Paper 99 (new edition); ISBN 0 255 36502 0
£10.00

Buckingham at 25

Freeing the Universities from State Control
Edited by James Tooley
Readings 55; ISBN 0 255 36512 8
£15.00

Lectures on Regulatory and Competition Policy

Irwin M. Stelzer
Occasional Paper 120; ISBN 0 255 36511 X
£12.50

Misguided Virtue

False Notions of Corporate Social Responsibility
David Henderson
Hobart Paper 142; ISBN 0 255 36510 1
£12.50

HIV and Aids in Schools

The Political Economy of Pressure Groups and Miseducation
Barrie Craven, Pauline Dixon, Gordon Stewart & James Tooley
Occasional Paper 121; ISBN 0 255 36522 5
£10.00

The Road to Serfdom
The Reader's Digest *condensed version*
Friedrich A. Hayek
Occasional Paper 122; ISBN 0 255 36530 6
£7.50

Bastiat's *The Law*
Introduction by Norman Barry
Occasional Paper 123; ISBN 0 255 36509 8
£7.50

A Globalist Manifesto for Public Policy
Charles Calomiris
Occasional Paper 124; ISBN 0 255 36525 X
£7.50

Euthanasia for Death Duties
Putting Inheritance Tax Out of Its Misery
Barry Bracewell-Milnes
Research Monograph 54; ISBN 0 255 36513 6
£10.00

Liberating the Land
The Case for Private Land-use Planning
Mark Pennington
Hobart Paper 143; ISBN 0 255 36508 x
£10.00

IEA Yearbook of Government Performance 2002/ 2003
Edited by Peter Warburton
Yearbook 1; ISBN 0 255 36532 2
£15.00

Britain's Relative Economic Performance, 1870– 1999
Nicholas Crafts
Research Monograph 55; ISBN 0 255 36524 1
£10.00

Should We Have Faith in Central Banks?
Otmar Issing
Occasional Paper 125; ISBN 0 255 36528 4
£7.50

The Dilemma of Democracy
Arthur Seldon
Hobart Paper 136 (reissue); ISBN 0 255 36536 5
£10.00

Capital Controls: a 'Cure' Worse Than the Problem?
Forrest Capie
Research Monograph 56; ISBN 0 255 36506 3
£10.00

The Poverty of 'Development Economics'
Deepak Lal
Hobart Paper 144 (reissue); ISBN 0 255 36519 5
£15.00

Should Britain Join the Euro?
The Chancellor's Five Tests Examined
Patrick Minford
Occasional Paper 126; ISBN 0 255 36527 6
£7.50

Post-Communist Transition: Some Lessons
Leszek Balcerowicz
Occasional Paper 127; ISBN 0 255 36533 0
£7.50

A Tribute to Peter Bauer

John Blundell et al.

Occasional Paper 128; ISBN 0 255 36531 4

£10.00

Employment Tribunals

Their Growth and the Case for Radical Reform

J. R. Shackleton

Hobart Paper 145; ISBN 0 255 36515 2

£10.00

Fifty Economic Fallacies Exposed

Geoffrey E. Wood

Occasional Paper 129; ISBN 0 255 36518 7

£12.50

A Market in Airport Slots

Keith Boyfield (editor), David Starkie, Tom Bass & Barry Humphreys

Readings 56; ISBN 0 255 36505 5

£10.00

Money, Inflation and the Constitutional Position of the Central Bank

Milton Friedman & Charles A. E. Goodhart

Readings 57; ISBN 0 255 36538 1

£10.00

To order copies of currently available IEA papers, or to enquire about availability, please contact:

Lavis Marketing
IEA orders
FREEPOST LON21280
Oxford OX3 7BR

Tel: 01865 767575
Fax: 01865 750079
Email: orders@lavismarketing.co.uk

The IEA also offers a subscription service to its publications. For a single annual payment, currently £40.00 in the UK, you will receive every title the IEA publishes across the course of a year, invitations to events, and discounts on our extensive back catalogue. For more information, please contact:

Subscriptions
The Institute of Economic Affairs
2 Lord North Street
London SW1P 3LB

Tel: 020 7799 8900
Fax: 020 7799 2137
Website: www.iea.org.uk